RURAL CHANGE IN MACHAKOS, KENYA

A Historical Geography Perspective

Marilyn Silberfein
Temple University

UNIVERSITY PRESS OF AMERICA

Lanham • New York • London

University Press of America,® Inc.

4720 Boston Way
Lanham, MD 20706

3 Henrietta Street
London WC2E 8LU England

Printed in the United States of America

British Cataloging in Publication Information Available

Library of Congress Cataloging-in-Publication Data

Silberfein, Marilyn.
Rural change in Machakos, Kenya : a historical geography perspective / Marilyn Silberfein.
p. cm.
Bibliography: p.
Includes index.
1. Machakos (Kenya : District)—Economic conditions. 2. Agriculture—Economic aspects—Kenya—Machakos (District). 3. Rural development—Kenya—Machakos (District). I. Title.
HC865.Z7M337 1989 338.1'096762'8—dc20 89–32248 CIP

ISBN 0–8191–7470–X (alk. paper)

All University Press of America books are produced on acid-free paper.
The paper used in this publication meets the minimum requirements of American National Standard for Information Sciences—Permanence of Paper for Printed Library Materials, ANSI Z39.48–1984. ♾

To the memory of my grandmother

Fanny Rudman Pershan

ACKNOWLEDGEMENTS

The initial research for this study was carried out with supporting grants from The Social Science Research Council and the National Geographic Society. Subsequent visits to Kenya were sponsored in part by Summer Grants from Temple University.

It would not have been possible to do this research without the encouragement and support of numerous Kenyans. I especially want to thank friends at the University of Nairobi: members of the Department of Geography where I was enrolled as a research assistant, Philip Mbithi of the Sociology Department, and the staff of the Institute for Development Studies. Other Kenyans also made important contributions including regional officials and members of the Ministry of Agriculture, Machakos District, the student assistants who carried out the surveys, and the many farmers who willingly shared information. Logistical support was made available by the African Inland Mission in Machakos and the family of Rhoda Zarembka in the Mua Hills. I look forward to the time when I can work with some of these people again.

The preparation of the manuscript was greatly facilitated by the late Professor David Sopher of Syracuse and Janet Crane now with the National Geographic Society who made many editorial suggestions. The research done by Derrick Thom as part of a USAID project was particularly useful as it provided considerable survey data on the semi-arid areas of Machakos. Also important was the survey research done by Dick Myers for another USAID study and the map of Ecoclimatic Zones in Machakos and Kitui District developed by Derrick Thom and Ted Bernard. The original version of this map appeared in the *Journal of Developing Areas*.

Some of the ideas presented in this study were first published in a chapter titled "Differential Development in Machakos District, Kenya," in *Life Before the Drought*, edited by Earl Scott. The publishers Allen & Unwin (now Unwin Hyman) have graciously given permission to reprint material from this chapter.

Getting the manuscript into finished form was a laborious task which required the help of several technical experts. Rita Jackson, now with the Math Department, Temple University did much of the original typing. For the past years, the various drafts have been prepared by Gloria Basmajian of Temple University's Word Processing Center. Her patience with my handwriting and frequent changes has been exemplary and the final product reflects her high standards. The maps were prepared by the Cartography Laboratory in the Geography and Urban Studies Department, Temple University, under the direction of Mark Mattson. The final maps for publication as well as photo layouts have been produced with great creativity by Yi Ching Chern who brought to this task professional experience with text preparation in Taiwan.

My final note of appreciation is reserved for friends and family members who refrained from asking when the manuscript was going to be finished and for my husband John Pawling who took all the photographs that are included in the text and who shared the special experience of doing research in Kenya.

TABLE OF CONTENTS

FIGURES

TABLES

PLATES

CHAPTER 1

INTRODUCTION

1. The General Context

The current agricultural crisis in Africa has finally captured the world's attention. There is now ample justification for concentrating research and resources on the African dilemma: rapid population growth combined with falling agricultural productivity that contrasts with rising crop yields elsewhere in the world. There is no easy remedy for this situation. The West has promised but not provided the financial support to deal with this crisis, nor has it acted to stabilize prices for African exports. Many African governments, on the other hand, have struggled to adopt the policy reforms (price incentives, increased budget allocations to agriculture, for example) that were to be their contribution to an improved environment for agricultural growth.[1]

This study provides a historical geography perspective on some of the issues behind the current impasse of population growth with stagnant or declining levels of crop output. The initial overview is followed by a case study of Machakos District, Kenya, an area which represents a median position with regard to access to resources, markets and infrastructure. The region was selected in part because it includes several distinct environmental sub-regions, making it possible to show changes in policies and responses across an ecological gradient.

Three factors in particular that have been implicated in Africa's agricultural decline will be discussed in general terms and then in the context of Machakos District: 1) the unique characteristics of the African environment, 2) the damaging impact on indigenous production systems of colonial occupation, and 3) the policies of independent African states.

2. The Antecedents of the Crisis

Well before the twentieth century, African agriculturists had developed an approach to food production which usually included the following characteristics:

- It was based on an appreciation of the holistic nature of the environment and the impact of any single activity on the rest of the system;

- It involved an approach to agriculture that was primarily extensive and conservationist, preserving soil fertility by allowing natural vegetation to regenerate on exhausted fields, enriching the soil with manure and compost on selected plots, and maintaining as complete a vegetation cover as possible;

- It required a high level of knowledge regarding local soil and rainfall and the plant varieties that could be combined in each location;

- It emphasized mobility and flexibility, the former exemplified by field dispersal and the occupation of new land, the latter by the staggering of crops across the cultivated area and through the growing season.

In the late 19th century, the values and goals of alien cultures were superimposed on established societies amidst clashes and subsequent accommodations. In rapid order the African population came to provide a product to the new colonial regimes, either labor or a surplus derived from agriculture or cattle keeping. Since African farmers and workers received only a small portion of the total value of their product, the exchange system ensured that most of them would become marginalized, unable to compete for fair compensation in the cash-based economy.

Two important themes run through this emerging relationship. The first of these involves the dismantling of indigenous modes of production and risk avoidance. In effect, while Africans were being excluded from full participation in commercial activities, they were also prevented by regulations and changing circumstances from realizing the potential of their own production system. Colonial administrators took no cognizance of the adaptive qualities of African agriculture; instead, they acted in ways that often disturbed the delicate balance of people and environment. They also created boundaries between ethnic groups or between Africans and European settlers that restricted mobility and trade. As a result, there was a reduction in the number of options that were available to secure survival within the subsistence system.[2]

The second theme is based on the creation of a new set of what might be called spatial conditions. As a result of differential access to the centers or colonial administration and economic activity, the African population was polarized. Areas that had once been complementary in terms of the mutually beneficial exchange of local products were transformed either into zones of investment, emerging commercialism, and economic differentiation, or zones or marginality, neglect and sometimes increasing impoverishment.

These themes persisted into the period of independence. They were, in fact, reinforced by an emphasis on industrialization that led to both an urban bias in the use of scarce resources and heavy taxation of the rural population. This mode of operation was not seriously questioned until the mid 1970s when the specter of land deterioration, decreasing yields, persistent poverty, and inequity became potent threats to state stability as well as to individual well-being. A reassessment of the rural development process took place at this point based on a belated recognition of the adaptive qualities indigenous production systems and on a revival of interest in more marginal or isolated areas. Thereafter, strategies designed to deal with the problem of agricultural or environmental decline have combined the experience and insights of African farmers with technologies introduced during the colonial and post-colonial period.

a. The African Environment

The tropics pose special challenges to cultivators and these have become more important with rapid population growth and increased commercial farming. Two factors are particularly significant in the African context, the unreliable rainfall and the frequency of poor quality soil. It is not actually the average annual rainfall that is critical but the probability of receiving a specific amount of rainfall in a given rainy season and the distribution of precipitation within that season. When the rains cease immediately after planting, for example, the result may be low rates of seed germination and the need for subsequent replanting; a shortfall later in the season can mean stunted plants and low yields. Furthermore, much of the rainfall arrives as abrupt heavy storms, a phenomenon which reduces the opportunity for moisture to seep into the ground and, in turn, increases run-off and erosion. As for soils, they tend to be hardened by exposure to sunlight, shallow and acidic with low clay content and excess (sometimes toxic) levels of iron and aluminum. Such soils are easily eroded and a have a low moisture-holding capacity.[3] Even more important, the ability of the soil to retain nutrients and bases is undermined by leaching and rapid removal of humus.

The effect of these environmental factors is intensified by other qualities of a tropical setting: high average temperatures that increase rates of evaporation, heavy cloud cover during the major period of plant growth, and an unchanging photoperiodicity that is an inhibiting factor in the growth stages of certain crops.[4] Similarly, it has been shown that the ratio of grain to straw for many grain crops is greater in areas that have cool nights and falling autumn temperatures.[5] The production systems that evolved in response to these environmental factors will be discussed at the end of this chapter.

b. The Colonial Interjection

By the second decade of twentieth century colonial governments had been established in most of Africa and several policies of these governments impacted negatively on both the environment and the indigenous modes of food production. The most immediate change was the creation of African reserves sometimes accompanied by the alienation of land to European settlers. The policy disrupted a previously fluid situation that had allowed for both the general expansion of cultivated land and the selection of dispersed sites for crops and pasture. As the process of colonizing new land was undermined, some areas rapidly exhibited signs of crowding while others remained sparsely inhabited.

The drawing of boundaries provided one example of an imposed scheme for organizing the landscape; another was the regrouping of homesteads in selected areas. One such intervention was the relocation of dispersed farmers in settlement clusters or villages, primarily to facilitate administration and control but rationalized in terms of providing amenities including schools, dispensaries, or a more dependable water supply.[6] Most of the artificial villages were abandoned by dissatisfied participants or continued on a very small scale. Later (post 1930s), efforts were made to revive the theme of resettlement for the purpose of tsetse fly control or economic development but most of these attempts were also unsuccessful.

A related and more widely documented aspect of colonial control was the absorption of Africans into the cash economy in ways that were invariably disadvantageous. The indigenous agricultural systems were burdened with additional demands as Africans were made to provide at least one of the following: 1) a surplus of locally grown foodstuffs, 2) an introduced cash crop, or 3) labor for sale at the marketplace. Whatever the form of exchange, the African role was such that both control and rewards were minimal. The limited income that was generated was in turn drawn upon for the taxes and duties that were rapidly imposed.

The impact of the colonial system depended in part on relative location.[7] The core areas of a colony usually included an administrative center, important towns and routes, as well as mineral resources and some fertile and/or accessible agricultural land. The African population of this area consisted of migrant laborers and farmers who grew commercial crops or surplus food crops alongside their subsistence holdings. The initial locational advantage of the cultivators was often enhanced as credit supplies, marketing activities, and extension services came to be concentrated in the core.

In the rest of the colonial territory, frequently referred to as the periphery, the primary source of income for Africans was a type of outmigration that incorporated young males and left women, children, and the elderly behind. In some colonies, farmers in the periphery were actually prohibited from participating in cash crop cultivation but were instead induced to sell their labor in the core.[8] This type of outmigration varied in its deleterious impact on source areas. When males were absent for several years, leaving behind a skewed population, it was often impossible to cope with the demands of the cultivation cycle or to maintain the existing infrastructure. Fewer hardships were created when migration was seasonal and coincided with a diminished demand for farm labor inputs. In either case, labor migration worked to the advantage of the colonial economic structure as it allowed the migrants to be compensated with low wages while their families survived by dint of their own efforts on their remote farms.[9] This system also made it unnecessary to provide for retired laborers as they were expected to return to the farms that had been maintained by family members through their absence.

For those who remained in farming, assistance from the colonial government was often both misguided and counter-productive. Agricultural advisors often advocated deep plowing (in spite of the fragile nature of the soil), the monoculture of cash crops (although such stands were liable to insect damage and left soil exposed), and intensification of cultivation (although labor shortages made such efforts unrealistic). Furthermore, advice was usually most appropriate for larger farmers in humid areas rather than for the typical smallholder in a semi-arid location.

Few colonial administrators recognized the inventiveness of African farmers. In Sierra Leone in the 1920s, officials were surprised to discover that farmers were actually carrying out their own field trials with local rice varieties in mangrove swamps. Eventually, these experiments resulted in higher yields than had been achieved in such areas of long term European involvement as India.[10] Occasionally an extension agent acknowledged that shifting cultivation and other practices made sense in terms of local conditions, but generally these sentiments were buried under the dominant theory that called for the duplication of mechanized, energy intensive monocropping in the tropics.

Because of their lack of insight into established production systems, colonial administrators continued to make the same mistakes. For example, in Sukumaland, Tanzania, farmers went along with government guidelines that called for pushing back tsetse fly infested bush because this activity fit in with local priorities. Destocking campaigns on the other hand, were much less successful since cattle played multiple roles within the society.[11] There were numerous such instances in colonial Africa when ignorance of local conditions and values led to non-cooperation and the failure of a development effort.

A further complicating factor, especially in Kenya, was the presence of a European settler population. Had the settlers not been able to establish a successful base for commercial agriculture, it is likely that African farmers would have been given more encouragement to diversify and improve crop yields. For example, during the first years of European colonization the African farmers were assisted by colonial officials in selling their surplus crops. Once the settlers arrived, however, they gradually came to monopolize available agricultural inputs and markets.[12] The settlers also agitated for policies that would increase the labor supply rather than those that would benefit the African farmers.[13]

When the settler role is examined in detail, it can be seen to have undermined both African subsistence and potential commercial agriculture. The land selected for alienation was often the best, leaving Africans to farm the less promising areas. The settlers also acted to secure substantial subsidies for themselves. They dominated marketing boards so as to protect their crop prices and monopolized food milling and credit systems.[14] They also obtained as high a proportion as possible of available resources to include agricultural inputs, rail and road linkages and extension officers. Yet, these and other services were financed in part by the taxes paid by the African population.

c. The African State

By the early 1960s most African states had become independent. From their inception, these states were beset by such external problems as the increased cost of oil, rising prices for manufactured goods, and decreasing compensation for crop and mineral exports. Other difficulties, however, have been the result of internal circumstances, particularly the higher expectations that the new governments generated but never had the capacity to fulfill. When resources proved deficient for satisfying popular demand for social services, jobs, and economic opportunity, governments looked to alternative mechanisms for generating income. Two common approaches, manipulating the local currency and borrowing from abroad, simply pushed African countries into an even deeper morass. Currently, there is considerable interest in attracting private overseas investment but potential investors continue to react negatively to what they perceive as an unfavorable business climate in Africa.

Political as well as economic setbacks occurred after independence. Most governments were frustrated in the task of building a national allegiance that could compete with the strength of ethnic affiliation. The lack of a strong national identity was then compounded by the in capacity of the state to control its citizens as in the case of boundaries that could be easily crossed for the purpose of smuggling or illegal entry. Even more significant to the issue of control have been the opportunities available to individuals who are dissatisfied with the rewards or the cash economy, especially in agriculture. They are able to bypass the state marketing system by trading in the black market or by moving back into subsistence production and providing for most of their own needs.[15] To date, the use of coercion as a technique for influencing these processes has not proved effective.

One means by which the state has attempted to assert its authority has been through the centralization of power. This process has sometimes included abolishing district and town councils or eliminating the right of local authorities to generate tax income of their own. The results of centralization policies have been negative: efforts to achieve genuine participation of rural people in the development process have been stymied and a wide range of services and types of infrastructure have deteriorated. In effect, the centralized bureaucracies established by most African states have not been able to provide for local needs nor to replicate the standards of management that are expected of long-established bureaucratic organizations.

In part to downplay their inherent weaknesses, most African governments have tried to divert attention to development issues. Elaborate plans have been drawn up detailing anticipated activities in every sector related to economic growth and/or the improved availability of basic goods. The "blueprint approach as it has been called, succeeded mainly in creating additional expectations that had to be scaled down. Furthermore, these annual plans concentrated on the urban/industrial sector with the expectation that investments in cities would spearhead growth in the rest of the economy. When the new urban economic activities proved to be inefficient, uncompetitive, or too capital intensive to provide many jobs, the growing but unproductive bureaucracies became the main sources of additional employment.

Throughout the initial planning period of the 1960s, little interest was shown in agriculture. Those programs that were supported usually favored the larger, richer farmers and the more well endowed areas, or they were large-scale enterprises such as state farms and resettlement schemes. The cost of these expensive programs was usually not justifiable in terms of either the added productivity or the increased income of the participants, yet they continued to be replicated. Part or the explanation for the ongoing interest in large schemes was undoubtedly the opportunity that they provided for more government control than was possible in established rural communities.[16]

Another policy that impacted negatively on agriculture was the maintenance of low prices on crops sold through official government channels. Food crop prices were kept depressed to satisfy the demand for cheap food in the cities. Export crop prices to farmers were also controlled so that as much as half the world market prices could be retained by the government. In effect, marketing boards were collecting a tax on agriculture that was severely reducing incentives to produce.[17] Only in those countries, including Kenya, where farmers had organized or were able to exert political influence, was a reasonable rate of return provided to cultivators. The more common pattern was for the government to extricate the maximum possible revenue from the farm sector.[18]

The effect on agriculture of government neglect and low produce prices was exacerbated by an educational system, inherited from the colonial period, that stressed skills appropriate to the limited urban job market. By the time students completed primary school they were imbued with a negative attitude toward the occupation of farmer while their highest approval was reserved for an urban office job. This distortion of priorities ensured that primary school graduates, and, even more definitively, secondary school graduates would leave the rural areas at their first opportunity. They were also joined by farmers with less schooling who were convinced that even a low-paying, unskilled job would be more remunerative than cash cropping. The flow of rural-urban migrants which began before independence gradually increased in scale, depriving rural areas of talent and manpower.

By the mid 1970s it was clear that a combination of the factors mentioned above: a problem environment, the colonial legacy, and misdirected policies on the part of new governments were leading to the stagnation or actual decline of agricultural production per capita. More resources obviously had to be focused on rural areas and the approach that was often followed at this time was Integrated Rural Development or IRD. This strategy was based on the premise that several interventions needed to be made simultaneously to effect any significant change. IRD also took into account the reality that foreign assistance could best be secured by identifying a clearcut, multifaceted project.

Unfortunately, IRD did not turn out to be a panacea. Specific projects were beset by problems that ranged from a lack of the managerial capacity to the waste of scarce resources. The projects were also characterized by a strong top-down orientation. Without the involvement of the proposed beneficiaries in planning and execution, the planners could ignore labor constraints and develop inappropriate technical packages.[19]

One major inadequacy in rural production systems was tackled by IRDs and other projects but with limited results, specifically the low levels of input use by smallholders. As of 1983, African farmers were using less than 10 kg/ha of fertilizer as compared to 41 kg/ha for Asia and 37 kg/ha for Latin America.[20] This figure reflects shortages of manure in areas without draft animals as well as limited supplies of crop residues (which are also in demand as fuel and fodder). The low utilization rate for imported inputs (improved seeds, better tools, etc.) is closely related to other factors such as the lack of reliable credit, storage, and delivery services.[21] When the arrival of inputs is delayed, any subsequent use of the inputs is less effective than it would have been with timely application.

3. The Way Out of the Crisis: A Preview

a. The African Approach to Cultivation

It is now widely acknowledged that the improvement of African crop production must be based on established farming systems that have to be understood in detail so that additional technologies and inputs can be grafted on to them. One critical aspect of these systems is their reliance on extensive modes of production that maximize security without jeopardizing the fragile resource base. This approach is effective as long as population growth is gradual and opportunities remain for the colonization of new land. Since such conditions did not always prevail in Europe and Asia, farmers on those continents found that substantial intensification was necessary (applying increasing amounts of labor or capital per unit of land) in order to raise productivity. In Asia this process was often associated with the emergence of large irrigation-based autocratic states while in Europe the three field system of crop rotation rather than irrigated agriculture became the basis of increasing crop yields per hectare.

In contrast, the predominantly rural African population was, until recently, provided with an adequate supply of foodstuffs with only limited intensification. The typical sequence was as follows: fields were cleared and burned, the resultant ash layer hoed into the soil and cultivation established on a given field until yields declined below an acceptable level, usually within 1 to 3 years, and new plots were prepared. The exhausted fields would then be left to revert to a natural vegetation, a process which built up the nutrient status of the soil and improved its physical properties. Within approximately 8 to 15 years, given sufficient rainfall and the absence of overgrazing, a fairly thick cover of bush vegetation would have reestablished itself. At this point, the land would again be cleared for cultivation, giving rise to a term widely used to describe this process: rotational bush fallow.

The extensive approach to cultivation in Africa reflected the ready availability of land, a need for flexibility, and a concomitant reluctance to develop fixed assets that might be destroyed by an environmental crisis or regional conflict. However, intensive methods were always applied on selected plots and became more important toward the late nineteenth century with growing population densities or political centralization.[22] Yet, even when states and proto-states developed they did not seem to make heavy demands on the peasantry that would have called forth substantial increases in production. Most rulers tended to restrict their requirements to a small tribute combined with occasional corvee-type labor or the provision of foodstuffs for the ruler's traveling representative.[23]

The techniques that were used selectively to augment productivity per unit area either increased the availability of nutrients to growing crops or delayed, sometimes indefinitely, the need to clear new fields. Parcels of alluvial soil along river banks and in moist depressions were cultivated continuously and were frequently used for such specialty crops as sugar cane. Household refuse was applied to enrich the soil in the vicinity of the homestead where a profusion of vegetables, fruits, and root crops would be grown. The fertility of the outlying fields might also be enhanced through the use of legumes and a system of intercropping that simulated crop rotation. There were further techniques that were less common such as the stall feeding of animals for manure collection and the use of crop residues for green manuring.

African farmers also maintained as complete a cover as possible over the soil surface. This was accomplished through mixed cropping, a technique which also maximized the use of soil nutrients, provided selective shading, spread the harvest over a longer period, discouraged weeds, and sometimes eliminated the pests that would have been drawn to a monocropped field. Ridging, the building of heaps, and the spreading out of crop residues were used to create an irregular surface, diminish erosion, and generally improve soil aeration. At the same time that these efforts inhibited erosion, they had the additional effect of improving the moisture holding capacity of the soil.

The staple crops grown by these methods varied along a moist-dry continuum from a combination of plaintain and root crops to a predominance of maize and pulses, and finally to some combination of millets and sorghums with decreasing amounts of maize. The role of cattle also changed along the wet-dry continuum, becoming relatively more important as precipitation declined.

Most of the traditional crops grown in Africa had generally changed in response to evolution and plant selection by farmers. For example, many crops had developed extensive root systems which increased the supply of nitrogen and moisture that they could extract from the soil. They had also come to be characterized by a high level of genetic variability within each species, a factor which cut down on pest damage (pests can decimate a genetically identical stand of plants) and improved the chances that at least some individual plants would survive a period of environmental deprivation.

Farmers were always experimenting with these different varieties, hoping to identify positive qualities such as drought tolerance or the ability to flourish in a specialized ecological niche.

In terms of the relationship of energy input to caloric output, the agricultural systems developed by Africans were efficient and highly flexible. These systems incorporated knowledge of micro-climates which was essential in determining sites for planting and for relocating or changing crop combinations as the weather fluctuated through the growing season. The overall goal was not to maximize yields in any one season, but to try to minimize risk by insuring that there would be at least some output in spite of the damage that might be inflicted by moisture shortfalls or other externalities.

In Kenya and other countries with large semi-arid areas, the most important environmental constraint has been the amount and distribution of precipitation. As a response to the threat of inadequate rainfall, most cultivators routinely utilized practices that would minimize the impact of a single season with insufficient rainfall to meet crop needs. It was a sequence of years with below average or with unusually erratic rainfall during the growing season that would call for a more complex set of adjustments.

At some point, a sequence of precipitation shortfalls of increasing magnitude came to be identified as a drought. The term drought clearly reflects a human element more than a strictly meteorological condition since the impact of below average rainfall will vary according to such factors as population density and local resources. One approach to establishing a typology of water shortfalls is based on a three fold division into 1) the national drought lasting two or more seasons with serious loss of production in two or more provinces, 2) the regional drought extending through one or two growing seasons and varying in impact with local conditions and 3) the one season local drought. On the continuum from regional to local drought, the frequency of drought increases (from an average of once every ten years to once every two or three years) while the size of the impacted areas decreases and tends to be confined to semi-arid ecological zones.[25]

The various devices used by African cultivators to deal with low levels of precipitation have been summarized by several authors. Three such attempts at identifying the regularities in the system of survival appear with occasional adjustments of order in Table 1.1. Each author's approach conveys the complexity and flexibility of the mechanisms available to the cultivator. The actual choice of options depends in part on two additional facets of the decision making environment: the relative availability of resources and 2) the severity of the drought situation.

TABLE 1.1

Modes of Coping with Precipitation Shortfalls
According to Three Major Sources

Mbithi & Wisner (1972)	Knight & Wood (1975)	Berry et al. (1971)
1. Affect RF source prayer, seeding	1. Hazard Modification a. More RF, prayer, seeding b. More water storage, irrigation	1. Adjustment affecting the basic cause of hazard: prayer
2. Increase availability of moisture	2. Systems Modification: plant early	2. Adjustments that modify hazard:
improve soil moisture storage and distribution, irrigation	cattle management	better utilize existing RF, high moisture soils, irrigation, ridging, plant early, weed thoroughly, space better
plant early, plant larger area, plant in moist spots	drought resistant crops, weed more thoroughly	
3. Reduce moisture need: drought resistant crops, weed more thoroughly	3. Risk spreading: social risk spreading	3. Modify loss potential of man and his work:
4. Accept or insure against loss: normal surplus, wage work, sell cattle, hunt, fish, non-farm activities	spatial risk spreading: scatter fields, part time work elsewhere, new colonialization	drought resistant crops
	temporal risk spreading: normal surplus	forecast warning, shift family to non-affected area, adjust diet to available foods
5. Distribute or share losses: ask help of kin, govt. etc., send children to kin, move to scheme	4. Migration	4. Adjustments that deal with losses by suffering them, planning or providing for them, or sharing them: alternative labor, invest in cattle
Do nothing		
	5. Let nature take course	

With regard to the first theme, it is clear that farmers with fewer resources cannot make optimum decisions. In effect, the poor often have to carry out actions that are critical to their immediate survival but that undermine their economic systems in the long run.[26] For example, in a study of seven years of water short fall in Ethiopia, there is a demonstration of the relationship between adaptive strategy and relative wealth.[27] After seven years of below average rainfall, the poorest families had exhausted both their own resources and all employment opportunities, and had migrated, died, or become completely dependent on relatives. At this point, intermediate families were beginning to face a serious threat to survival, having utilized a change of agricultural practices, sale of commodities and land, local employment, and some interdependency (in that order) as means of coping with disaster. The wealthier families, however, were still in possession of disposable resources (land, cattle, or other possessions).

The second theme, the relative severity of the water shortfall, has been examined in some studies but usually in terms of a basic two-fold division. At one end of the spectrum are the methods for dealing with minor, recurrent fluctuations in precipitation which usually become institutionalized. In contrast, extreme environmental conditions cannot be accommodated and require substantial changes or emergency measures.[28] In reality, however, there are several levels of adjustment between the two extremes and these often grade into one another as a crisis becomes more severe. Using the Kamba as an example, a complex sequence of adaptations to drought can be discerned in at least four spheres of activity: 1) the agricultural system proper, 2) the carrying out or established rituals, 3) participation in supplemental (non-agricultural) pursuits, and 4) the use of staggered mobility. Each of these will later be discussed in depth.

Although agriculture and supplementary pastoral activities were of paramount importance in nineteenth century Africa, individuals invariably engaged in additional occupations. In Kenya, for example, metal working, brick-making, pottery working, salt collecting, beer brewing, charcoal preparation, and weaving were all important economic activities. As the amount and variety of fabricated goods increased, and as awareness spread of the range of agricultural products available in Kenya's diversified environmental setting, a greater impetus was given to the development of exchange networks and specialized trade. A final group of functionaries included administrators and individuals with skills in healing, in predicting the future, and in interceding with the supernatural.

b. New Insights and Their Application

The negative attitude toward African farming that was so obvious a part of the colonial record persisted into the independence period. When farmers reacted unfavorably to government projects it was considered indicative of conservatism in the face of technical change. Only gradually did it become obvious to administrators that African farmers were inventive and responsive to opportunities and that their rejection of an intervention usually implied that it was inappropriate given local constraints and priorities.

By the 1970s new approaches to extension and the improvement of productivity were being designed although the degree of interest varied from one country to another. These approaches were based on the proposition that if farmers were going to modify their proven farming systems, it would require innovations that would 1) provide rapid and viable results, 2) increase the reliability of the food supply, and/or 3) be applicable at a time in the planting cycle when labor constraints were not already high. When necessary, these efforts could be tied to input supply or marketing schemes in support of the original effort.

Unfortunately, viable agricultural innovations with the characteristics described above have rarely been available. There are no technologies or varieties that will automatically translate into substantially higher yields. This situation contrasts with the Green Revolution in Asia, where hybrid varieties of rice and wheat are cultivated with fertilizer, usually under conditions of controlled moisture. This approach cannot readily be transferred to Africa, however, since African farmers often lack access to fertilizer, draft animals, a dependable supply of labor or spare cash, all items that tend to be available to Asian smallholders. Furthermore, in the Asian lowlands there are large areas that are environmentally uniform and it is common to grow just one or two irrigated, staple crops, unlike Africa with its more varied environment and its emphasis on multicropping and rain fed agriculture.

Improving agricultural productivity in Africa in the near future will require new approaches. Plant breeding may be important, but it will have to be conducted with and understanding of past problems. Promising hybrids that have already been introduced failed because they were less pest resistant, less competitive with weeds, or less able to produce without inputs than the local varieties.[29]

Agronomic research will also have to be oriented to more than just the humid regions. Most successes in African plant breeding to date have focused on humid areas, especially where input supplies and markets have been readily available. For example, in 1977 half of the maize growing smallholders in the Kenya Highlands were producing high yielding varieties (HYVs).[30] Similarly, the spread of HYVs in the higher rainfall areas of Zimbabwe has been facilitated by having a private company provide the seeds.

In contrast, the semi-arid areas of Africa have suffered from both difficult physical conditions and inadequate research. The first agricultural center to focus on the drylands was located in India and the crops that were developed there proved intolerant of the more extreme African conditions. Particular problems were encountered with sand in the Sahel, erratic rainfall, and distinctive pests.[31] It was not until 1981 that the African drylands research center known as ICRISAT was founded in Nigeria, although even ICRISAT was slow in designing trials that replicated real farm conditions rather than ideal circumstances. As a result of all these delays, improved varieties of such drought-tolerant crops as sorghum or pigeon peas are just being made available to farmers.

The research frontier has now reached a point where there are two major goals in addition to creating new varieties: 1) incorporating environmental preservation into the development process and 2) integrating HYVs with the prevailing agricultural systems and conditions. It is the conservation component which poses the greatest challenge. The current wisdom is to build on indigenous techniques for erosion control and for improving the fertility, structure, and moisture-holding capacity of the soil. One such approach calls for higher levels of recycled crop residues. Tests done in Ibadan, Nigeria have shown that mulching increased crop yields by 25 to 60 percent.[32] Secondly, legumes can be increasingly incorporated into the intercrop in order to take advantage of their nitrogen-fixing capacity. Related to this activity is alley cropping, alternating rows of crops and rows of trees, especially leguminous trees. Branches can be cut back during the rainy season to provide organic material and fodder.[33] The ideal tree for this purpose and one that has been used by African farmers in the past is Acacia Albida which has a nitrogen fixing capacity and which loses its leaves during the rainy season--providing mulch around the new crops at the same time that it eliminates the problem of overshading. Thirdly, water supplies must be used more effectively, in part by decreasing runoff. Mulching and terracing are helpful in this regard but there are several supplemental techniques such as the building of microcatchments by scooping out small depressions in which water can accumulate and gradually sink into the soil. Even the ridges constructed to reduce slope erosion can retard water flow sufficiently to intensify infiltration. Beyond this level, there is need for small scale channel-based irrigation which is more labor demanding and not yet common in Africa.

The other area where research needs are critical is in the integration HYVs or new technologies and practices into ongoing farming systems. A key line of investigation is the relationship of crop yields to fertilizer application. Inorganic fertilizers, in addition to being expensive and difficult to supply, have been shown under certain circumstances to contribute to soil acidity. Furthermore, individual crops vary in their response to nitrogen, phosphorous and other minerals, making it difficult to add a single mineral blend to an intercropped field. Instead of emphasizing mineral fertilizers, it makes sense to experiment with organic materials as well as developing crop varieties with low fertilizers needs. Some plants of this type are already available such as fonio which is known to provide a reasonable yield in areas with poor quality soil.[34]

Farming systems research in Africa invariably calls for a focus on the overall productivity of an intercropped field rather than on single crops in isolation. It has actually been shown that in the context of African agriculture, increasing specialization in a single crop may actually correspond to a decline rather than an increase in productivity since these crops tend to be more subject to such problems as pest damage and to provide less plant residues for soil fertility.[35]

Once new varieties or technologies are available, they need to be distributed to the rural population. This process is expedited when farmers are organized in such a way that information goes out from the extension staff and positive as well as negative reactions come back, allowing for design changes. Furthermore, both research and extension activities have to be planned in the context of environmental conditions and farming systems that can vary from one locality to another, each calling for specific technologies and seed combinations. Some strategies for dealing with this complex reality have already been devised, such as the spreading out of seed multiplication sites to ensure that experiments will take place in appropriate settings for a large number of potential users. In effect, interventions have to be introduced carefully in response to local assessments of environmental conditions, relative access, and the resources of the farmers themselves.

c. The Specific Context: Machakos District, Kenya

All of the issues discussed above are going to be viewed from the perspective of a single group, the Machakos Kamba. These people have proved to be very resilient, devising techniques for surviving in a semi-arid environment as well as methods for augmenting resources through trade and cattle keeping. All of these strategies were damaged by the foreign occupation and much of this study is related to the stages during which accommodations were made to this new reality.

During the first period of contact with the British, the Kamba staged numerous attacks on military and trading posts, reacting first to the East Africa Company, and then to the newly appointed officials of Kenya colony. Military action on the part of the colonial regime ended these outbreaks and paved the way for more serious incursions: land alienation of European settlers and the imposition of an extensive system of taxation. By the end of World War I the colonial administration was firmly in control. At this point it was already clear that the Kamba system of production was being adversely affected by land confiscation and recruitment of Kamba men as laborers for expatriate farms and government public works projects.

The inter-war period was characterized by a consolidation of the earlier gains by both the colonial government and the settler population. Africans were no longer able to compete as cash crop farmers, instead they were left with the options of employment for low wages or food production on holdings that were dwindling with rapid population growth. This was also an era in which famine and land deterioration were referred to with increasing frequency and in which regional differentiation was firmly established. The highlands which had received the bulk of investment in both infrastructure and services had become dominant in terms of income, opportunity, and accessibility. The lowlands, in contrast, remained isolated sources of migrant labor unable to generate any local commercial activity.

The colonial government was eventually forced to reassess its development strategy as a result of the declining quality and availability of land and the resurgence of organized African political activity. Two experimental programs were launched in the 1950s, ALDEV and the Swynnerton plan, one of which focused on food crops while the other provided selected Africans with a role in commercial agriculture. Both of these approaches achieved some of their goals, but they were not able to correct regional inequities or find long term solutions for problems of land deterioration.

The period leading up to and following independence (1960-1974) was characterized by numerous experiments in agricultural development but none of them were able to change the basic patterns that had already been established. Lowland and highland remained disparate even as the downslope flow of land-poor farmers created population concentrations in drought-prone areas. Options for small holders were further restricted as access to such necessities as land, water, and firewood increasingly came under private control. A concerted effort to deal with these issues did not emerge until the mid 1970s when the government finally began to reexamine the original Kamba system of survival, including its emphasis on anticipating moisture shortfalls and on regional interdependency.

CHAPTER 1: REFERENCES

[1] Morello, Ted. "U.N.'s Recovery Program Fails to Make Dent in Crisis." *The Christian Science Monitor*, Nov. 6, 1987.

[2] O'Keefe and Wisner, "African Drought," 35.

[3] Ter Kuile, "Humid and Subhumid Tropics," 101-103.

[4] Dommen, *Innovation in African Agriculture*, 9-10.

[5] Chang, "Tropical Agriculture, Crop Diversity and Crop Yields," 247.

[6] See, for example, J. McKay. 1968. "A Review of Rural Settlement Studies of Tanzania." *The East African Geographical Review* 6:37-49, or R. B. Dakeyne. 1962. "The Pattern of Settlement in Central Nyanza, Kenya." *The Australian Geographer* 8:183-191.

[7] Soja, *Political Modernization of Kenya.*

[8] Arrighi, "Labor Supplies in Historical Perspective."

[9] Cliffe, "Underdevelopment or Socialism," 115.

[10] Richards, *Indigenous Agricultural Revolution*, 25.

[11] Brandstrom, "Development Efforts in Sukumaland," 47.

[12] Brett, *Colonialism and Underdevelopment in East Africa*, 173.

[13] Ruthenberg, *Agricultural Policy in Kenya*, 36.

[14] Leys, *Underdevelopment in Kenya*, 36.

[15] Hyden, *No Shortcuts to Progress.*

[16] Hart, *Political Economy of West Africa Agriculture*, 87.

[17] Bates, *Markets and States in Tropical Africa*, 30.

[18] Hinderink and Sterkenberg, "Agricultural Policy in Africa," 20.

[19] Richards, *Indigenous Agricultural Revolution*, 38.

[20] Harrison, *The Greening of Africa*, 83.

[21] Blackie, "Restructuring Marketing Systems," 187.

[22] Several studies have attempted to quantify the relationship between population growth and agricultural intensification. These include: John Levi. 1976. "Population Pressure and Agricultural Change in a Land Intensive Economy," *Journal of Development Studies* 13:61-78 and B. L. Turner, R. Q. Harnen, and A. V. Portarro. 1977. "Population Pressure and Agricultural Intensity." *Annals of the Association of American Geographers* 67:384-396.

[23] A good discussion of this topic can be found in Catherine Coquery-Vidrovitch. 1976. "The Political Economy of the African Peasantry and Modes of Production." In *The Political Economy of Contemporary Africa*, ed. Peter Gutkind and Immanuel Wallerstein. Beverly Hills, California: Sage Publications.

[24] Dommen, *Innovation in African Agriculture*, 11.

[25] Wisner, "Overview of Drought in Kenya," 6-8.

[26] Hill, *Development Economics on Trial*, 22.

[27] Wood, "Farmers' Responses to Drought," 82-85.

[28] Mbithi and Wisner, "Drought and Famine in Kenya," 15.

[29] Dommen, *Innovation in African Agriculture*, 18.

[30] Harrison, *The Greening of America*, 102.

[31] Ibid., 99.

[32] Ibid., 107.

[33] Okali and Berry, "Alley Farming in West Africa," 1.

[34] Timberlake, *Africa in Crisis*, 150.

[35] Dommen, *Innovation in African Agriculture*, 119.

CHAPTER 2

MACHAKOS DISTRICT: THE PHYSICAL AND CULTURAL SETTING

1. Machakos District as a Physical Region

The focal area of this study is a composite of highlands and lowlands which currently covers approximately 14,000 Km^2. The base rock throughout tends to be pre-Cambrian, primarily gneisses and schists, but there are limited areas of other rock such as dolomites and volcanic lavas.[1] The physiognomy of the region is shown on Figure 2.1 which confines itself to the drainage system of the Thwake River (outlined on Figure 5.1). Almost all of the colonial territory of Machakos District lies within this drainage basis which consists primarily of incised seasonal streams in which dry season water can usually be found beneath the sandy stream bed.

The highlands of Machakos District contain four major hill massifs (Iveto, Kangundo, Mbooni, and Kilungu) that reach up to over 1824 meters (600 feet). These massifs and the smaller hills that lie between them include both gentle and steep slopes, the latter often taking the form of rock outcorps with sharp ridges. The hills stand on the average 609 meters (200 feet) above the surrounding basins which in turn vary in elevation from 912 to 1216 meters (3000 to 400 feet).

The predominant gneisses and schists of Machakos have weathered into soils that vary in texture according to their position on an undulating surface. In moist depressions, the soils are relatively fertile but because they are sometimes waterlogged they can be difficult to cultivate. On foot slopes the predominant type is clay-loam which is fairly well drained but which tends toward high acidity with low levels of organic matter. These soils can also form a hard surface when dry.[2] On the higher slopes, soils are well drained but sandy and often shallow in depth.

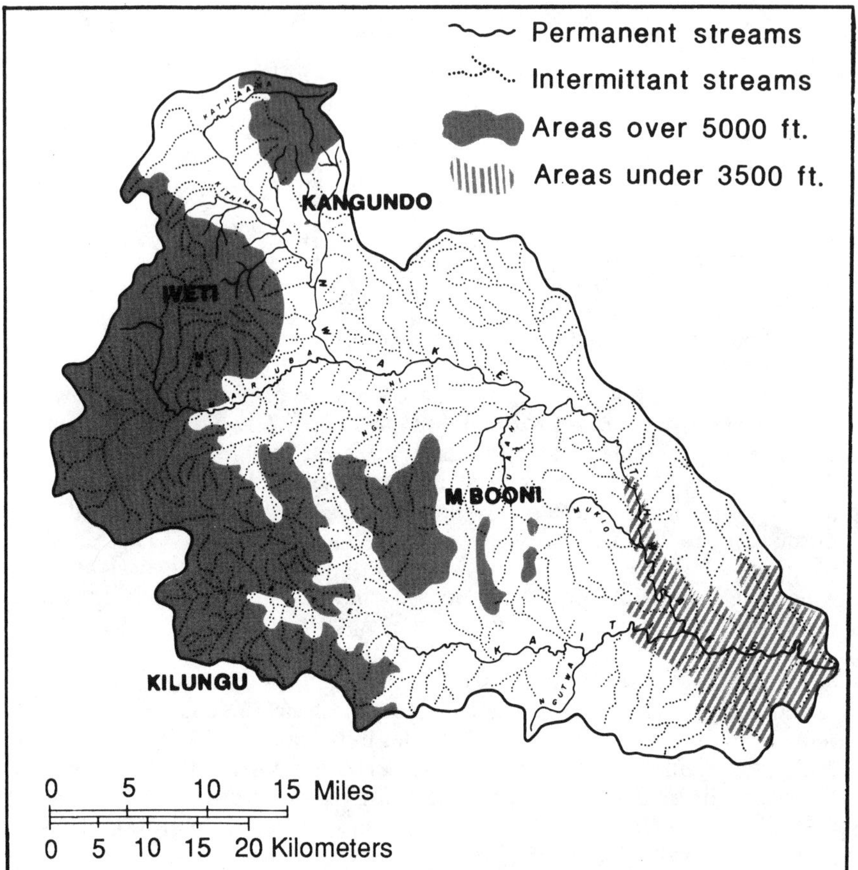

Source :

Machakos sheet, 1:250,000 GSGS 4672, 2nd edition, british war office, 1953.

Figure 2.1 Elevation

As soil analysis has become more sophisticated and thorough in this region, it has been possible to compile maps and diagrams that group soils on the basis of their suitability for agriculture. One such classification systems recognizes four soil capability types based on drainage, depth, organic content, position on a slope, and texture.[3] The best soils are found on the intermediate slopes and lowlands of the western part of the district while the category that ranks second in quality predominates throughout the eastern lowlands. The poorest soils are usually found on the higher slopes of the massifs.

The other important facet of the Machakos physical environment is climate, particularly precipitation regimes. Additional aspects of climate such as radiation, temperature, humidity, etc., create spatial patterns that are too detailed for the current scale of coverage.[4] Rainfall in the Machakos area follows a bimodal equatorial pattern with two distinct dry seasons separating a maximum in October-November (short rains) and in March-April (long rains). Average annual rainfall varies from over 1000 mm in the northern hills to under 500 mm at lower elevations in the far south.

During both rainy seasons, the distribution of rainfall is subject to considerable fluctuation that is unpredictable in the short run. The highly variable long rains fail 30 percent of the time as compared to 10-20 percent rate for the short rains.[5] Furthermore, precipitation is often received as localized, heavy storms which produce rapid run-off, erosion, and subsequent loss of soil moisture. The situation is exacerbated if, as is often the case, evapotranspiration levels are high. In much of Machakos District, potential evapotranspiration is exceeded by rainfall only in April and November.[6]

The impact of this type of rainfall distribution on agricultural activities is substantial. Even if rainfall totals are adequate for a particular crop, there may be critical times, such as the early growth phase of a plant, when a discontinuous moisture supply can lead to problems of wilting, stunting and, ultimately, decreased yields. For example, a two-week delay in the onset of the rains beyond the optimum planting time, can result in a substantial decline in yields.[8] Precipitation also varies in total amount from one year to the next as evidenced by a sample of rainfall statistics from Machakos town (Table 2.1).

The spatial variation in the distribution of rainfall coincides with the topographic divisions of the region. The highlands are characterized by a higher average and greater reliability of rainfall than the lowlands. In addition, the highlands tend to have higher potential photosynthesis as a result of cooler overnight temperatures (slowing down plant respiration) and a longer growing season that reflects both radiation and rainfall regimes.[9]

TABLE 2.1

Average Annual Precipitation At Machakos Town, 1909-1939*

1909-10 - 868.7 mm (34.2")	1925 - 845.8 (33.3)
1910-11 - 777.2 (30.6)	1926 - 1018.5 (40.1)
1911-12 - 1394.5 (54.9)	1927 - 1477.0 (58.15)
1912-13 - 1356.4 (53.4)	1928 - 587.5 (23.13)
1913-14 - 767.1 (30.2)	1929 - 747.0 (29.41)
1914-15 - 848.4 (33.4)	1930 - 1283.2 (50.52)
1915-16 - 713.0 (28.2)	1931 - 1110.2 (43.71)
1916-17 - 124.9 (49.2)	1932 - 1099.8 (43.3)
1917-18 - 901.7 (35.5)	1933 - 937.3 (36.9)
1918-19 - 889.0 (35)	1934 - 703.6 (27.7)
	1935 - 876.3 (34.5)
	1936 - 1028.7 (40.5)
1922 - 1072.9 mm (42.24")	1937 - 1247.1 (49.1)
1923 - 1155.7 (45.5)	1938 - 757.4 (29.82)
1924 - 77.2 (30.4)	1939 - 532.9 (20.98)

*Based on data from 1894 to 1977, Machakos station has a mean annual precipitation of 946 mm with a range of 457 to 1,585 mm and a standard deviation of 260 mm (Moore, 1979:419-20).

The rainfall pattern of Machakos District is also reflected in the distribution of natural vegetation. In the nineteenth century it is likely that a predominantly evergreen forest covered the higher slopes of Machakos District, grading into a mixed forest and then a combretum woodland on the middle and lower slopes. By the beginning of the colonial period some slopes had already been cleared of their original forest cover to be replaced by a combination of scattered clumps of trees, bushy growth, and frequent clearings. Some of the highest slopes were covered with bracken and grass which were said to absorb and retain all available precipitation.[10]

The vegetation of the low lying areas was a mixture of herbaceous plants, scattered trees, and deciduous thornbush in varying proportions. When cattle grazing was extended onto the lowlands the thornbush, often infested by tsetse flies, was pushed back. Thus, the frontier between the varying vegetation types changed position frequently with the vicissitudes of local conflict, climatic variation, changing population densities and, ultimately, the colonial influence.

Various attempts have been made to combine precipitation and other characteristics of the physical environment into a schema that would provide a zonal classification system for Machakos District. In a 1953 report, L. H. Brown identified ecological zones based on combinations of natural vegetation and the expected carrying capacity.[11] In a later publication, Brown devised land classes that included average annual rainfall, slope, soil and cultivation characteristics and then estimated the maximum population density that could be supported in each land class without leading to soil destruction or famine.[12] There were several problems with this system: it was sometimes based on crude data and it took into account only average total rainfall figures without reference to rainfall distribution or potential evaporation rates.

A more meaningful approach to identifying environmental zones was incorporated into the "Land Potential Statistical Abstract" of 1972 and later refined in the Kenya Soil Survey. The method is based on the ratio of annual rainfall to annual potential evapotranspiration. The latter factor, which represents the total moisture which would be transpired from a continuous plant cover of known height, was estimated by Penman using such information as temperature, wind speed, and reflecting radiation.

The zones that are usually identified using this approach range from I to VI, and of these, four are of particular interest in Machakos District. They are shown on Figure 2.2 which is based on a map designed by Bernard and Thom. Zones II, III, and part of IV, which correspond to the highlands, are areas of relatively dependable rainfall, usually more than 875 mm (35 inches) a year. In Zone II, rainfall is at least two thirds of potential evapotranspiration, and in Zone III, at least one half (moisture index does

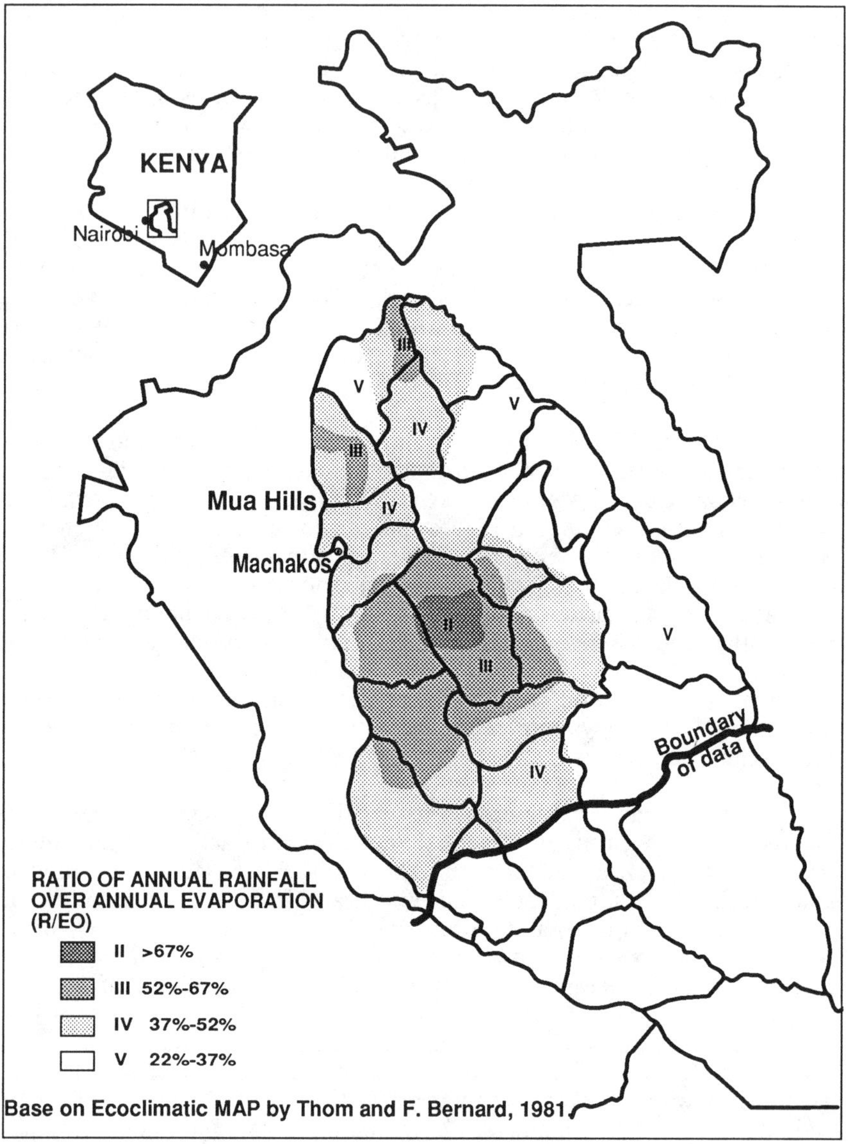

Figure 2.2 Ecoclimatic Zones

not exceed -30). These climatic conditions, combined with the appropriate soils, are considered to provide a medium to high potential for agriculture and to be suitable for intensive livestock management with a carrying capacity of less than 2 hectares per stock unit.[13] Zone four, also known as the semi-arid area (low to medium potential), is characterized by average rainfall figures of approximately 525 to 850 mm. The figure of 762 mm (thirty inches) annual rainfall is an important one since this amount is often considered crucial for unirrigated agriculture.[14] The total annual rainfall is, in turn, one third to one-half of evapotranspiration (moisture index of -30 to -42). Under these circumstances, the most successful agricultural activities are based on rapidly maturing or drought resistant crops to include sorghum, millet, sisal, Katumani maize, etc., or on livestock production with two to four hectares required per stack unit. Zone V, or the arid area, has a moisture index of -42 to -51 whereby rainfall is approximately one fourth to one-third of the evapotranspiration total. These areas are suitable to agriculture only where fertile soil is combined with available surface water or above average precipitation. There is some rangeland potential but per-unit stock needs exceed 4 ha.

2. The Occupation of the Land

There is still some controversy as to the original migration route which led the Kamba to Machakos but, when the evidence is pieced together, it points to a southern source region. Legends, linguistic material, and other ethnographic information give credence to the hypothesis that the Kamba migrated from northeastern Tanzania, probably in the 1500's (Figure 2.3).[15] They first occupied the plains north of Kilimanjaro, an area without a dependable water supply, and not well suited to permanent agriculture. Their movement toward the hill masses of Machakos may have been accelerated by an increasingly inadequate land base or by Maasai, competition, but whatever the motivation, they seem to have passed Kibwezi and the Chyulu Hills and reached Nzaui by the 1600's.[16] When this area proved to be unsatisfactory (poor soil and insufficient protection were important limitations) the migration stream continued north, reaching the Mbooni Hills in about 1650.[17] In this propitious setting, where fertile soil and adequate rainfall were combined with protection from external forces, the Kamba moved into a more settled phase using root crops and legumes to establish a successful extensive agriculture.[18] Over the following century the gentler slopes and valleys of Mbooni were filled by settlers who began the process of modifying the environment to suit their needs, damming streams and occasionally building terraces.

Early in the eighteenth century, contingents of Kamba began to move out from the hills into the surrounding territory. One group crossed the Athi River, possibly as an extension of seasonal movements, and established itself in Kitui.[19] Shortly thereafter, another segment, avoiding the drier

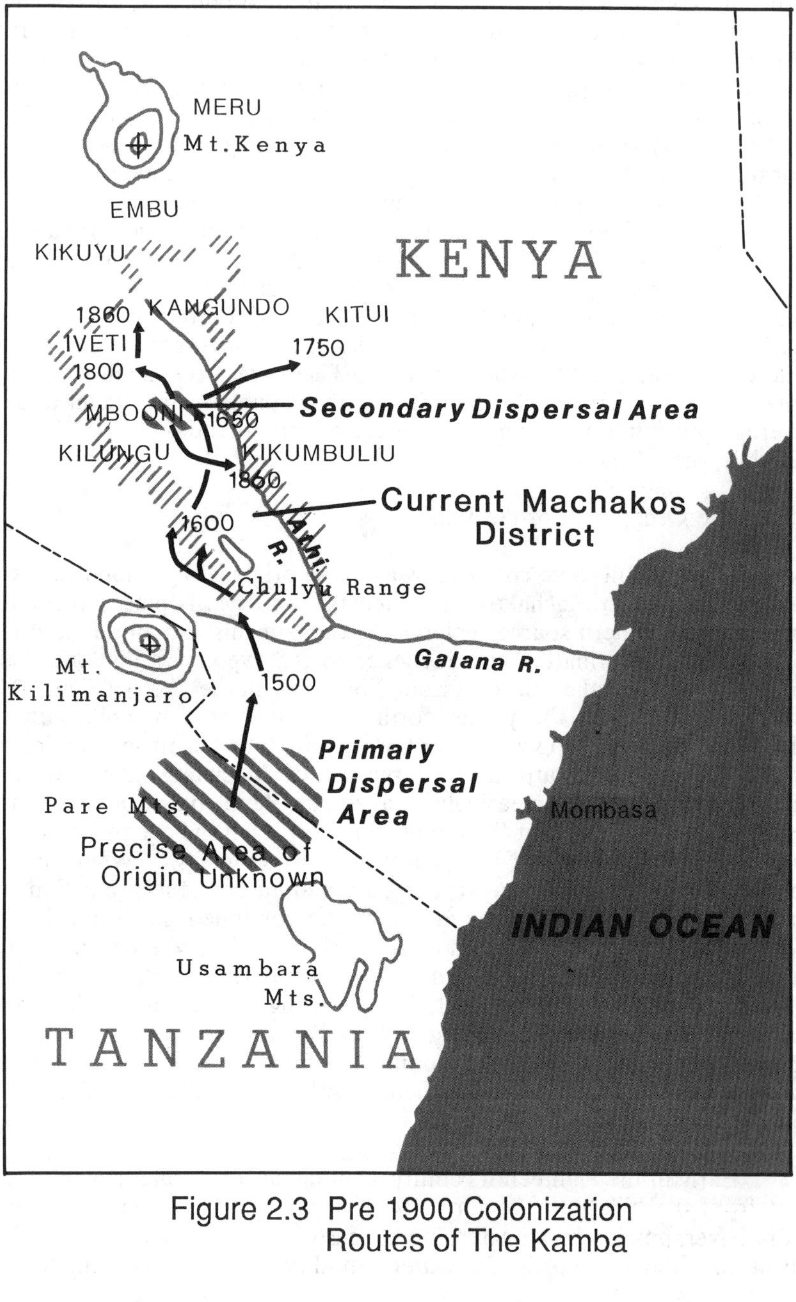

Figure 2.3 Pre 1900 Colonization Routes of The Kamba

plains, moved southwest into Kilungu. A northerly expansion was also initiated, probably by 1800, into the Iveti hills and neighboring areas.[20] By the time of the British intervention, the Kamba were moving into two pioneer zones: one in the north (Kangundo, Matungulu), and one in the south (Kibaoni, Kikumbuliu).[21]

The reasons for the migrations out from Mbooni after over a century of settlement in the area were probably similar to those which had brought about earlier relocations. Population growth in the Mbooni Hills must have caused at least local destruction of the soil base. Conflicts between clans or individual families over land, leadership, or other factors were undoubtedly a stimulus to colonization. It is also possible that a more pastoral way of life, similar to the system that prevailed when the Kamba were in the Kilimanjaro area, may have begun to reestablish itself.[22] It is clear that there was no single explanation for the diaspora and that groups of varying sizes subsequently moved out from Mbooni. Some of these were able to resettle peacefully, while others, encountering competitors such as the Galla, had to carry out raids or defensive measures to protect their frontier.

At the same time that the Kamba were dispersing longitudinally, they were oscillating between the higher and lower slopes of the occupied hill masses. Homesteads were usually located at higher elevations where both water and security from the rival Maasai were more readily available. During the day individuals moved downslope to herd cattle or to cultivate some of the wetter locations along stream courses. At night, lookouts were assigned the task of watching for Maasai bands from sentinel hills.

The entire colonization process, involving both long and short distance relocation, was shaped by the Kamba social and economic structure. Relocation usually resulted when the growing population of a homestead (*musyi*) could no longer be provided for within the constraints of an extensive cultivation system. At this point, it was common to assign to the oldest son the responsibility of finding and occupying a new holding (*Ngundo*), demarcating its boundaries, clearing the fields, and initiating cultivation. He and his descendants would then have rights to this piece of land in perpetuity.[23]

While the relocated family was establishing itself, cattle would be grazed on the uncultivated portions of the cleared field. When a herd became too large for this practice, cattle were shifted to the commonage (*weu*) which was used jointly by all the cattle owners in the vicinity. Some individuals fenced off portions of the *weu* to create a family cattle post (*kisese*) but upon abandonment, this land, unlike the cultivated fields, reverted to the *weu*.[24]

When the original settler decided that his new situation was satisfactory, other brothers might locate nearby as space allowed. It was customary for the youngest son to stay behind with his parents and eventually to inherit the original family homestead. On the other hand, should the oldest son be dissatisfied with his original choice of a relocation site, he had the right to return to his father's land or to select a new destination. This process was facilitated by the practice of allowing a migrant son to continue to cultivate at least the more desirable irrigated plots he had left behind and thus preserve his interest in the original family holding.[25] Furthermore, whenever a piece of land attached to the original homestead was redistributed, it was considered necessary to consult all closely related kin. In practice, a migrant would be expected to show an interest in the activities of his parents' homestead, but such involvement gradually ceased among his children or grandchildren.[26] Thus, opportunities to return to an area of origin tended to lapse after the second or third generation.

This system of colonization was effective since land was usually readily available, but several factors could complicate the procedure. For example, a short term imbalance of land and population could still take place, especially during years of below average or poorly distributed rainfall. Another source of disruption was the occasional conflict over high quality land. It was the frontier situation itself that posed the greatest threat, however. Both groups and individuals might be overwhelmed by droughts, floods, insect infestation, competition, or unexpected conditions that would reduce their numbers before a retreat could be carried out.[27]

The existence of these hazards frequently caused would-be migrants to look for alternative strategies to relocation. Tenancy was one of the options available to someone whose family plot was already thoroughly subdivided but who preferred not to migrate to the frontier. Land could be leased from a neighbor on condition that the property would revert to the first owner upon repayment of the original fee.[28] The owner was supposed to give sufficient notice upon reclaiming a plot and allow the tenant to keep possession of a crop that was already in the ground.

One end product of the process of colonization described above was the creation of a decentralized political structure based on spatially dispersed clans. Clan membership remained significant for such matters as land adjudication, although, in practice, close contacts were normally not maintained beyond the extended family. In terms of day-to-day social interaction, the locality group (*utui*) and its council of elder males (*kisuku*) was most significant. The settlement unit of the *utui* could best be described as a hamlet of scattered homesteads, often occupying an interfluve between seasonal streams. The members of the group, invariably representing more than one clan, would assist each other as the need arose. For example, the ten to twenty-five adult males of an *utui* would frequently join together as a *Mwethya* group to carry out a particular task such as housebuilding. Several *utui* would, in turn, form a community (*kibalo*) which would function as a looser unit than the *utui* in order to facilitate social interaction (with its own men's club and frequent marriages), defense, or the preparation of large scale sacrifices.

Beyond the kibalo, units of association were not identified in terms of specific, area-based institutions. Interaction continued to occur on an irregular basis in connection with special events such as initiation dances, warfare, regional marketing, long distance trade, mutual assistance and, infrequently, disputes over territory. It is a distinctive characteristic of the Kamba that these forms of interaction were able to take place without the creation of a centralized authority structure.[29]

3. Drought and The Strategy for Survival

The regional mobility of the Kamba was a product of recurrent water shortfalls as well as the colonization process. A combination of Kamba oral history and data from the early colonial period confirms the occurrence of large scale droughts and related famines at ten-year intervals. The initial period is cloudy, but there were probably two famines between 1800 and 1830: one called the "staggering famine," because of the unusual gait induced by hunger, and the second called the "scorched skull" famine.[30]

By the time of the third famine (1836), a more accurate dating is possible. It was known as the "famine of disappointment" and probably resulted in a resettlement of some Kamba in a better watered coastal zone at Rabai. In the early 1850's the "long famine" caused the explorer Van der Decken to avoid going inland as conditions were considered too precarious.[31] In 1862 the famine of "pounding skins" took place followed in 1871 by widespread food shortages and a substantial movement of Kamba families out of the district. A subsequent drought of unknown date was called "to bleed cattle" because cattle-blood became an important source of nourishment.[32]

A very severe water shortage known as the "famine of the star" (probably named after a comet seen in that year) was reported on by Thompson as he travelled through parts of Kamba territory.[33] Then, after a relatively long period without a disastrous scarcity of food, "the famine of rice" (this being the only food available) took place in 1898-99).

The recollections of groups and individuals seem to have been particularly vivid in the case of severe famines. Survivors have described the destructiveness, the social trauma, and sometimes the emergence of raiding parties and brigands, all leading to a general insecurity in the countryside.[34] There were far more minor than major shortages during this one hundred year period since they caused less calamity, their detailed descriptions did not survive as well through the medium of oral history.

Some of the techniques used by the Kamba for coping with varying degrees of water shortfall are contained within the description of particular droughts. As was suggested earlier, however, the various modes of ensuring survival can be systematically organized according to activity type and the severity of the water shortfall. These approaches will now be elaborated on, assuming again a range of situations from average conditions to several consecutive seasons of rainfall deficit.

A. The Agricultural Continuum

In preparation for a typical planting season, Kamba farmers frequently incorporated practices which would improve the chances of an adequate harvest should precipitation fall below expectations. One such practice was the planting of drought-resistant crops including millet, sorghum, and certain legumes (pigeon peas, for example). Intercropping was often carried out so as to form a complete vegetative cover over the soil (taller plants shading lower ones and reducing evapotranspiration), and to insure a diversity of crops so that at least some plants would ripen during low rainfall years. Some farmers built ridges, in part to improve the capacity of the soil to store moisture.[35] They would also try to get at least some crops into the ground before the first rains so as to take advantage of the season's full moisture supply and the flush of soil nutrients following the beginning of the rainy season. Subsequent plantings might then be staggered in keeping with an erratic rainfall pattern. During those years when the moisture needs of the crops were met, a surplus of food would be produced that could be used as a reserve against future shortages.

Whenever possible, Kamba farmers tried to take advantage of ground and surface water supplies. Streams flowing out of hilltop springs were sometimes diverted into fields and planting was carried out in natural moist depressions.[36] In drier areas water was obtained by digging wells into dry river beds. It was also common for farmers to keep cattle as part of their reserve assets.

Whenever a water shortage persisted beyond a single season, greater emphasis might be placed on the techniques mentioned above at the same time that additional practices were incorporated into the agricultural system. Early and staggered planting became more essential as did reliance on drought resistant crops. The total area cultivated might be expanded to include all available moist depressions and it was likely that weeding would be carried out more thoroughly in order to cut down on wasteful transpiration. Some farmers would adjust the spacing of their crops (especially millet and sorghum) in order to maximize moisture utilization.

Finally, cattle would be increasingly relied on as a direct source of emergency foodstuffs and as a commodity that could be traded for other dietary requirements.

This description conveys the action-pattern of a hypothetical farmer, but in reality there were departures from this sequence as a result of variations in elevation and resources. Families living in the higher, better watered areas could rely on adequate rainfall during most seasons, while those in the lowlands needed to be better prepared for water shortfalls. Access to resources, especially labor, was another critical factor. Any effort invested in forestalling drought-related famine might have to be withdrawn from alternative activities. The growing of millets and sorghums, for example, required that family members guard against bird damage to the crops. The building of ridges and the cultivation of heavy, waterlogged soil would also be labor-demanding.[37] Alternatively, the cultivator with substantial supplies of seed or cattle might neglect some labor-intensive techniques in favor of consecutive plantings or reliance on potential cattle sales. In essence, the selection of practices and the precise order in and which they would be implemented would be expected to vary according to micro-habitat, relative labor and material resources, and the meteorological conditions prevailing over the previous few years.

B. The Ritual Continuum

An ongoing and complex system of rituals provided another mode of coping with the threat of drought. The focus of the rituals were *N'gai*, the creator and supreme being, and the *Aimu*, or spirits of the departed.[38] Both elements of the supernatural were associated with the availability of precipitation. While *N'gai* could control the amount of rainfall, the *Aimu* functioned as predictors of future events. They had no fixed location, sometimes dwelling in the underworld, but they frequently visited the land of the living. Some were nasty and destructive, but many were sympathetic, taking on a punishing role only when they were critical of the conduct of selected humans, or when they felt neglected.

Both *Ngai* and the *Aimu* could be appealed to through the ritual of sacrifice. The *Aimu* of a particular household would be provided with small amounts of food on a regular basis. In exchange, they would be asked for specific types of assistance, such as an estimate of the amount and distribution of precipitation for the coming season. Not everyone could communicate with *Aimu*--the most likely recipients of information being specialized functionaries or *Mwathani*. Such individuals have often had a very high measure of success in prediction and undoubtedly supplemented their supernatural sources with insights into subtle meteorological phenomena and other appropriate signs (animal behavior being one).

Whatever the capacity of a given community to predict precipitation, it was particularly important to have a direct influence on rainfall availability by virtue of sacrifice to *Ngai*. This practice could be traced to a myth whereby the first drought to beset Ukambani resulted from a failure to perform sacrifices.[39] Ritual slaughter of farm animals (usually oxen, goats, sheep, or chickens) took place at regular intervals during the agricultural cycle to coincide with such activities as planting, harvesting, and thrashing and to insure their success.

The scale of sacrifices and related activities increased whenever scarcity threatened. From simple ceremonies involving just a few individuals, they would be expanded to include most residents of a community and the designation of specialized roles. The following description conveys the organization of a Kamba sacrifice made during a period of drought:

> The women are put in charge of rainmaking activities because of their dominant role in cultivation. All the mothers meet at sunset, to beat the drums and dance until midnight at the medicine woman's hut. In the morning, after young men have danced around the door, a few old men come to the door and are told to take a goat to the place of sacrifice. A community procession follows them and witnesses the sacrifice of the goat. The final activity calls for the blood of the goat plus some sugar bean to be poured at the sacrifice site.[40]

At the center of the event was a healer (*Mundu Mue*) whose roles included that of community priest, medical diagnostician, prescriber of curative herbs, and general futurologist.

The actual sacrifice site also exhibited a range of types and locations. Many of the rites that reoccurred regularly throughout the year would take place at the homestead near a particular tree or pile of rocks. A large-scale sacrifice, however, would take place at a community shrine (*Ithembo*) which was usually a large fig tree or groove of trees, often located on a hilltop. The selection of new *Ithembo* sites took place as the Kamba expanded and specific sites were chosen because of the unusual size or shape of local trees or because of proximity to the graves of important figures. Some *Ithembo* acquired particular importance as a result of legends that were associated with them or special accomplishments resulting from local sacrifices. For example, a large Python was said to reside at one *Ithembo*, his benevolence being assured by the gifts of milk and ghee that were donated by the local people.[41]

To summarize, the ongoing provision of food (in the case of the *Aimu*) and regular sacrifices (to *N'gai*) represented attempts to maintain good relations with the forces beyond Kamba control. When extreme events occurred, however, as in the case of a drought, the scope of the sacrifice changed along with the need to remove any source of displeasure to *N'gai*. Large scale community rituals came to prevail, with widespread participation. Some of the more important *Ithembo* sites were used and large animals (a goat as opposed to a chicken) were incorporated into the ceremonies. These activities were beneficial in that they increased the confidence of the community in supernatural intervention, alleviated the psychic suffering that was bound to accompany a threat to one's livelihood, and often allowed individuals to devote more energy to constructive pursuits.

C. The Continuum of Supplementary Activities and Interdependence

Although the focus of Kamba economic life was agriculture and cattle keeping, homesteads were organized so as to allow alternative activities to be pursued, usually on a part-time basis. Women were frequently engaged in the production of various crafts and pottery as well as brewing beer and bee keeping. For men, hunting provided a basic source of supplementary foodstuffs or income. The Kamba hunt actually existed at two levels--in part it involved pursuing animals that would provide a source of meat and skins, but a specialized contingent of hunters concentrated on the elephant in order to acquire valuable ivory tusks. Other specialized types of production included the preparation of arrows and poisons, both of which were widely regarded and copied.[42] Iron ore, much of it collected from stream beds, was processed in small forges with charcoal and used to produce ornaments, spears, and knives.[43]

The products of small scale manufacturing as well as these derived from the agricultural, pastoral, and hunting sector of the economy formed the basis of trading networks. Since the Kamba territory included several ecological settings, it was possible to take advantage of the variation in food production over short distances. For example, fruits or vegetables produced in the hills might well be exchanged for cattle products derived from lowland pastures.

Trading systems appear to have expanded to a regional scale, around 1800.[44] The Kikuyu were the outstanding trading partners although the Embu and Mbeere undoubtedly participated as well. The Kamba were a source of arrow poisons, other medicines, hides, gourds, and sometimes iron ore or craft items.[45] The Kikuyu, especially during the period of early trade contact, were most likely to export yams, grains, and other foodstuffs, until they developed their own processed goods.

The hunting skills of the Kamba were a major factor in their participation in a further sphere of activity: long distance trade. They were well located for such an occupation, considering their proximity to sources of ivory as well as to potential trading partners on the coast (Arabs and Swahilis). They were also able to use their contacts with such neighboring groups as the Kikuyu and the Embu to obtain additional ivory and related trade goods. Special techniques and devices were developed to assist in long distance travel, including sandals designed to protect the feet against thorns, a portable fire-making device, and a type of heavy rope that could be used in crossing a stream.[46] Members of trading caravans also became proficient at providing security as they ventured into increasingly distant territory.

One particular attraction of this type of trade was that it did not necessarily disrupt the cultivation system. In central Tanzania, for example, Nyamwezi carriers were able to join the caravans on the central Tanganyika routes for much of the year, but they invariably returned home during peak periods in the agricultural year.[47] A similar report on Kamba traders indicates that it was not until the maize harvest was complete that the ivory caravans would form.[48]

By 1840, it was common for Kamba caravans to reach the coast on almost a weekly basis carrying such goods as ivory, poison for arrows, and cattle products which they would exchange for cloth, beads, copper, and salt.[49] Unfortunately, the Kamba position began to deteriorate shortly thereafter as a result of both the hunting out of local and adjacent territory and a change in Swahili trading patterns to a more southwesterly direction.[50] This route change was feasible because the Swahili had dissipated the Maasai threat at about the same time that they had gained sufficient knowledge to be able to operate on their own in the interior.[51]

As a result of these setbacks, the Kamba were forced to develop new trading strategies. They tried to find outlets for such commodities as rhino horn and local medicines.[52] They also reached further into the interior in their quest for ivory; some of their caravans being reported north of the Tana River and beyond Marsabit (Figure 2.4).[53] By the 1870's, the Kamba were once again playing an important role in the long distance trade, in part as middlemen between the Swahili and their sources of goods to the north and west of Machakos.

Many dramatic accounts have emerged of Kamba trading and hunting expeditions. Krapf's journals include the description of a caravan that went far into Tanzania and actually reached the country of the pygmies near Lake Tanganyika.[54] Krapf was sufficiently impressed with the trading prowess of the Kamba to make the following comment: "It was our wish to visit in the interior those Wakamba who--traversing as they do for trading purposes a large section of East Africa--may well claim the most serious attention of a missionary."[55] Kamba traders had also been able to set up small colonies among the Sambaa in the Usambara Mountains of Tanzania where they functioned as middlemen in regional trade and utilized their widely acknowledged skills as elephant hunters.[56] Both Sambaa and Pare traditions point to the presence of Kamba traders in their respective territories in the

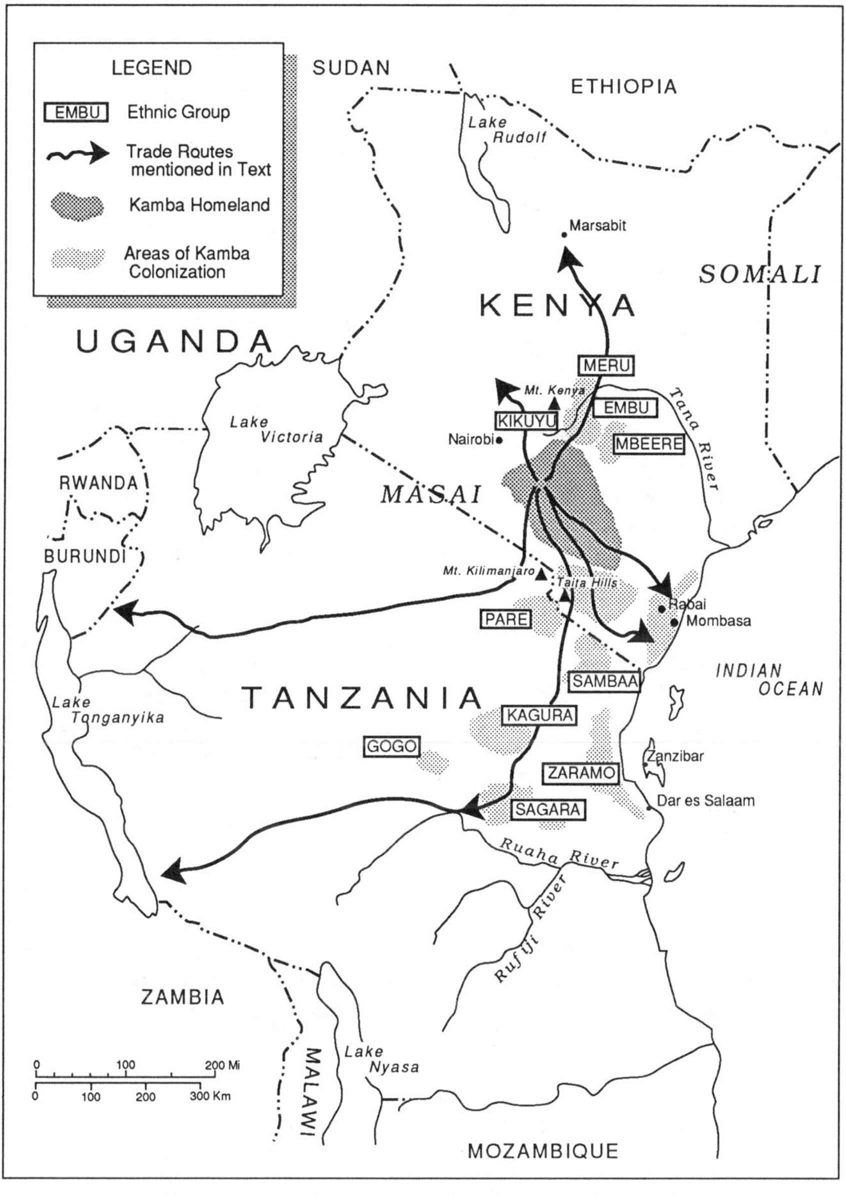

Figure 2.4 Areas of Kamba Trade and Drought Related Migration

mid-eighteenth century, but there is currently no evidence from the Kamba legend that would corroborate such early relocations.[57]

The range of activities discussed above became more significant when drought threatened the production of food crops. Women could expand their non-agricultural activities and both men and women could engage in the production of bricks and charcoal to be sold or exchanged for foodstuffs.[58] Women would also have the major responsibility for obtaining supplementary foods that were not usually present in the Kamba diet such as fish, wild fruits, berries and roots. It was the individual with hunting and trade experience who was most likely to increase his effort at this time. Caravans continued to function even in periods of drought and participants in the trading network could usually find purchasers or employment, and thus obtain currency for foodstuffs.

During times of stress it was also possible to activate trade networks for the provisions of mutual assistance. Participants in the long distance trade might be able to acquire emergency food supplies from the coastal areas, parts of which had become important grain production centers.[59] Local trading relationships were also important--farmers in the better watered highlands often providing foodstuffs for their more vulnerable lowland counterparts.[60]

Networks based on kinship provided another source of assistance. Ties between clan members were maintained by visits during the dry season although the web of relationships might break down as distances increased.[61] These linkages could also form the basis for exchanges of needed foodstuffs when conditions deteriorated. The Kamba tradition of reciprocity and the sharing of scarce resources facilitated assistance to the hardest hit farmers during a drought.

D. Staggered Mobility

The final aspect of the Kamba strategy for survival is related to their capacity to move over long distances. Numerous references have been made to Kamba mobility as traders and in one discussion they are referred to as "a culture on the move--which spread from Machakos to Kitui, from hills to plains, from one ecological site to another."[62]

The most basic form of the mobility strategy, however, did not involve migration or long distance trade, but instead was based on field dispersal. Most farmers maintained fields at more than one topographic elevation for several reasons. Crops were likely to have better yields on the higher slopes in response to more reliable rainfall but the quantity of this type of land was limited, and could only be supplemented by lowland cattle pasture and fields--especially those lying near water courses. In the drier areas, field dispersal provided added insurance that a below-normal yield on one plot might be balanced by adequate productivity on another field. It was also possible to disperse cattle among relatives in different ecological zones with the expectation that at least some of the sites would provide adequate pasturage.[63]

Field dispersal gradually graded into the satellite-farm mode of cultivation whereby an additional plot was opened at a distance from the main fields which precluded daily visits. A designated family member would usually maintain this outpost during the peak-labor period to ensure a supplemental food supply in the event that drought, insect infestation, or another short term crisis undermined production on the primary plot.

Field dispersal can be regarded in part as an adjustment to the expectation of a one or two season precipitation shortfall. The mobility strategy could be expanded if this approach, along with the appropriate agricultural activities, rituals, and systematic sharing were inadequate. Adult males could look elsewhere for hunting and trading opportunities or for farm work. As a drought situation worsened, the next stage might be to send children away while parents attempted to salvage a meager harvest. Relatives living in better-watered areas were most likely to receive the children, but even such neighboring groups as the Kikuyu might accept limited numbers of outsiders who were willing to work in exchange for food.

Under the most extreme condition, whole families were forced to relocate, sometimes over long distances. As a rule, such movements were temporary, but they became permanent when subsequent obstacles made it difficult to return, or when members of the original party made conscious decisions to relocate as a result of perceived opportunities in the recipient areas.

When possible, designated individuals within local communities were assigned the task of searching for resettlement sites among alternative locations. The Kikuyu area, higher and less dry, was one possibility, although there was relatively little open space for settlement in the highlands and always the chance of strong resistance to outsiders.[64] The coastal region provided other potential locations for resettlement. There are records of a Kamba party reaching the area around Rabai during the famine of 1836--a group that was later observed by Krapf on one of his early treks through the Kenyan hinterland.[65] Invariably, some of the drought-related settlements were reinforced by Kamba trading parties and some came to function as entrepots along the major routes to the interior.

The most impressive concentration of Kamba settlers outside of their homeland emerged in northern Tanzania, an area stretching from the Usambara and Pare Mountains to the Zaramo territory on the east and to

Usagara in the south (Figure 2.4). The settlements were described by German travelers of the late nineteenth and early twentieth century who attributed their presence in the region to a sequence of drought-related migrations. Once the initial colonies were established, smaller detachments penetrated further south until some vanguard groups of Kamba hunters had reached as far as central Tanzania.[66] Again, traders and hunters probably augmented the initial population of these small colonies and provided some ongoing links with the homeland. According to a representative of the Church Missionary Society, many of the Kamba in Tanzania would have returned to their hills, but their routes were blocked by Maasai clans ("the fierce, nomadic Baraguyu") and, consequently, they stayed on in Usagara and its environs.[67]

The reception of Kamba migrants in their destination areas varied from neutral to openly hostile depending on such factors as local population densities and previous efforts to penetrate the overflow region. One documented encounter took place between a group of Kamba fleeing from a famine (about 1900) and the Mbeere peoples to the northeast. Since the Kamba immigrants were rather aggressive, the Mbeere fled to Embu country--only to be pursued there as well.[68] Finally, the Kamba were pushed back across the Tana River after having brought about a full scale retaliation.[69] Another hostile encounter took place when some of the Tanzania Kamba tried to conquer a piece of Kaguru territory in the late 1880's, but the Kamba were defeated and forced to retreat to the north.[70]

By and large The Kamba were able to coexist peacefully with neighboring peoples and often assisted in such functions as warding off the Maasai, obtaining trade goods, hunting wild game, and, occasionally mediating in local disputes. Yet, in spite of these various forms of interaction, the Kamba maintained their language and cultural institutions and continued to live in distinctive communities. Their identity as extra-territorial Kamba was reinforced by trading contacts with other members of their group as well as by sporadic visits to their homeland. The migrants were sometimes referred to by Machakos Kamba as those who have followed the rain.[71]

The strategy of migration as a mode of coping with drought has usually been equated with the most extreme actions utilized to survive famine, and has been criticized as being excessively disruptive.[72] It is certainly true that relocation can be a traumatic process conducive to increased levels of disease and mortality. In the context of the pre-colonial mode of adjustment, however, migration can be seen as the logical culmination of a series of actions that relate to movement or dispersal, to be applied only when conditions had badly deteriorated.

CHAPTER 2: REFERENCES

[1] Moore, "Erosion in Machakos," 419.

[2] Ibid., 420.

[3] Bernard and Thom, "Population Pressure in Machakos," 391.

[4] For additional information see Agency for International Development, Report No. 4, *Kenya: Arid and Semi-Arid Lands*, 2.2-2.6.

[5] Lynam, "Analysis of Population Growth," 73.

[6] Moore, "Erosion in Machakos," 420.

[7] Chang, "Tropical Agriculture," 248.

[8] Moore, "Erosion in Machakos," 419-420.

[9] Porter, *Food and Development in East Africa*, 22.

[10] Colonial Office, Kenya Colony, R. O. Barnes, *Memorandum on Soil Erosion*, 1.

[11] Colonial Office, Kenya Colony, L. H. Brown, *Agricultural Problems and Potentials.*

[12] Colonial Office, Kenya Colony, L. H. Brown, *National Cash Crop Policy*, 50.

[13] Pratt and Gwynne, *Rangeland Management*, 55.

[14] Baker, "Drought in East Africa," 171.

[15] Jackson, "Kamba Pre-Colonial History," 175-177.

[16] Lindblom, *Akamba of East Africa*, 125.

[17] Lambert, "Land Tenure Among the Akamba," 130-13.

[18] Jackson, "Kamba Pre-Colonial History," 178.

[19] Larby, *The Kamba*, 7.

[20] Colonial Office, Kenya Colony, *Machakos District Gazetteer*, 30.

[21] Oliver and Mathew, *History of East Africa*, 414.

[22] Jackson, "Kamba Pre-Colonial History," 202.

[23] Penwill, *Kamba Customary Law*, 32.

[24] Lambert, "Land Tenure Among the Akama," 143.

[25] Penwill, *Kamba Customary Law*, 43.

[26] Lambert, "Land Tenure Among the Akama," 57.

[27] Jackson, "Kamba Pre-Colonial History," 214.

[28] Penwill, *Kamba Customary Law*, 48.

[29] Oliver, "Individuality and Cultural Flexibility," 421-422.

[30] Lindblom, *Akamba of East Africa*, 339.

[31] Krapf, *Travels in Eastern Africa*, 339.

[32] Forbes-Munro, *Colonial Rule and the Kamba*, 22.

[33] Thompson, *Through Masailand*, 573-575.

[34] Jackson, "Pre-Colonial History," 239.

[35] Mbithi and Wisner, "Drought and Famine in Kenya," 15-16.

[36] Larby, *The Kamba*, 20.

[37] Wisner, "An Overview of Drought in Kenya," 42.

[38] Mbiti, *New Testament Eschatology*, 137-139.

[39] Ndeti, *Elements of Akamba Life*, 29.

[40] Beresford-Stoke, "Akamba Ceremony," 139-140.

[41] Ndeti, *Elements of Akamba Life*, 86.

[42] Orde-Brown, *Vanishing Tribes of Kenya*, 152.

[43] Gregory, *Great Rift Valley*, 349.

[44] Jackson, "Kamba Pre-Colonial History," 209.

[45] Lamphear, "Kamba and Mrima Coast," 81.

[46] Lindblom, *Akamba of East Africa*, 345.

[47] Kjekshus, *Ecology and Economic Development*, 182.

[48] Last, "Journey to Nguru Country."

[49] Kimambo, "Economic History of Kamba," 81.

[50] Lamphear, "Kamba and Mrima Coast," 99.

[51] Low, "Northern Interior," 317.

[52] Jackson, "Kamba Pre-Colonial History," 222.

[53] Lindblom, *Akamba of East Africa*, 12.

[54] Krapf, *Travels in Eastern Africa*, 302.

[55] Ibid., 283.

[56] Feierman, *The Shambaa Kingdom*, 126.

[57] Ibid., 127.

[58] Mbithi and Wisner, "Drought and Famine in Kenya," 16.

[59] Wisner, "Man-Made Famine in Kenya," 4.

[60] Porter, "Environmental Potentials," 419.

[61] Larby, *The Kamba*, 7.

[62] Oliver and Mathew, *History of East Africa*, 425.

[63] Mutiso, "Machakos Political Evolution," 2-3.

[64] Low, "Northern Interior," 314.

[65] Krapf, *Travels in Eastern Africa*, 256-257.

[66] Beidelman, "Notes on Kamba District," 186.

[67] Watt, *The Heart of Savagedom*, 52.

[68] Saberwell, *Political System of the Embu*, 42.

[69] Mwaniki, *History of the Embu and the Mbeere*, 29.

[70] Beidelman, "Notes on Kamba District," 188.

[71] Watt, *The Heart of Savagedom*, 259.

[72] Mbithi and Wisner, "Drought and Famine in Kenya," 20.

CHAPTER 3

THE ESTABLISHMENT OF MACHAKOS DISTRICT, KENYA COLONY

1. The Initial Contact Phase

The British East Africa Company (I.B.E.A.C.) organized the first long-term intrusion into the Machakos area in 1889 when they established a supply station for their planned foray into Uganda. The site of the station, present day Machakos town, was chosen because of its position along an established route not far beyond the point where that route left the dry Nyika plateau. The site had also gained some renown as the residence of the widely respected Kamba leader, Masaku.

Without any serious dislocation, I.B.E.A.C. was able to substitute for some of the trading ties that had already existed between the Kamba and the coastal Swahili, providing jobs for porters and purchasing local produce. The first stage of the British-Kamba encounter was interrupted, however, by an aborted revolt (1890-91) and, later, by an actual attack on the station. Tensions had resulted from the insensitivity of several I.B.E.A.C. officials to established Kamba prerogatives in the Machakos area. Another source of contention was the growing military strength of the supply post which included both British and Sudanese soldiers.

When John Ainesworth became the new company commander in 1892, relations improved temporarily, as did trade opportunities for the Kamba. This was also a period of increased British control over the neighboring Maasai, a situation which allowed the Kamba to expand the grazing to some of the adjacent lowlands that were previously Maasai dominated.

The influence of I.B.E.A.C. never extended very far beyond the site of Machakos. No attempt was made to establish British authority elsewhere in the district until it became clear that company government was to give way to some form of colonial administration.[1] Similarly, the company made few attempts to analyze or influence local social and economic conditions as long as they could obtain needed supplies and laborers. Isolation from the indigenous population was exemplified by Ainesworth himself who maintained a garden near his home for experimenting with tropical crops, but showed no interest in local agricultural practices.[2]

With the establishment of the British protectorate in 1895, Ainesworth moved to enlarge his sphere of responsibility to include all of the newly created district. In essence, his goal was to eliminate slave and cattle raiding while expanding the British zone of control; first to the northern frontier area where additional posts were built, and then later to the south.[3] The situation in the north became critical almost immediately as the Kamba of the Mwala area responded to outside interference by burning a British post. A punitive expedition stifled this revolt but only by using Maasai to supplement the British contingent.[4] Other areas were subdued with less destruction until, in 1897, local feuds provided the British with an excuse to intervene in Kilungu where earlier fugitives had often retreated.

This confrontation marked the end of the period of primary Kamba resistance.[5] Several factors had undermined their capacity to withstand the expanding British influence and control. A severe famine during 1898-99, complicated by disease, rinderpest and locust attacks, rendered the local population particularly vulnerable. Nor had the Kamba ever joined together in a common enterprise that would have prepared them to confront the current intruders with a united front. Finally, some areas of Machakos District were isolated from these early encounters, while others (particularly the Iveti Hills) had well established trading ties with the colonial government and remained neutral throughout the period of conflict.

When the military situation became less critical, colonial policies were devised and implemented among the reluctant Kamba that were to create long-range problems for the district. A hut tax was introduced in 1901 that was transformed into a tax on all adult males when numerous huts were found empty at collection time. Since these administrative changes required improved territorial demarcation, the northern part of the district was divided into locations, each of which corresponded to between two to twelve communities (*Ivalo*) and often to a distinct physical region such as a hill massif. By 1910 there were seventeen locations, two of which, Manyalla and Kithangaini, were amalgamated in 1925 to form Maasii (Figure 3.1).

At about the same time the hut tax was being imposed, land was being opened to European settlement (Figure 3.2). The Crown Lands Ordinance of 1902 included a plan for long-term leases, initially for 99 and later for 999 years. By 1906 the Athi and Kapiti plains west of Machakos had been set aside for British settlers and the Yatta Plateau to the east had been similarly

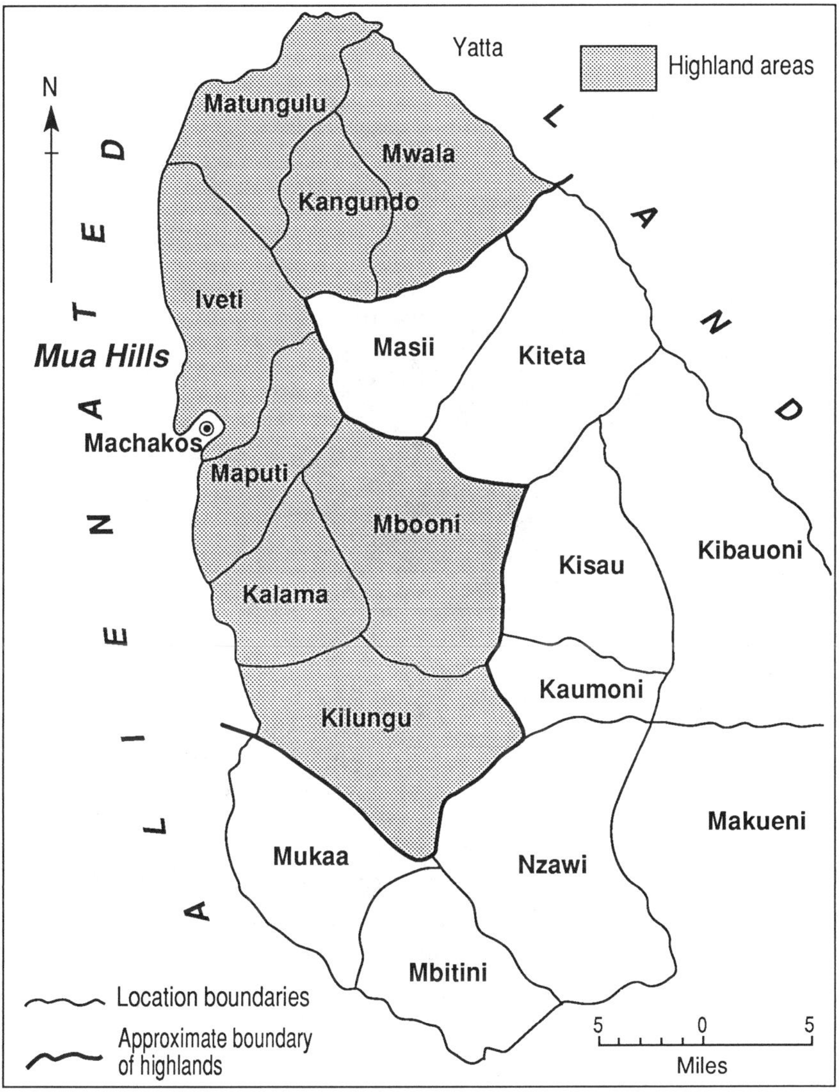

Figure 3.1 Administrative Divisions: 1930

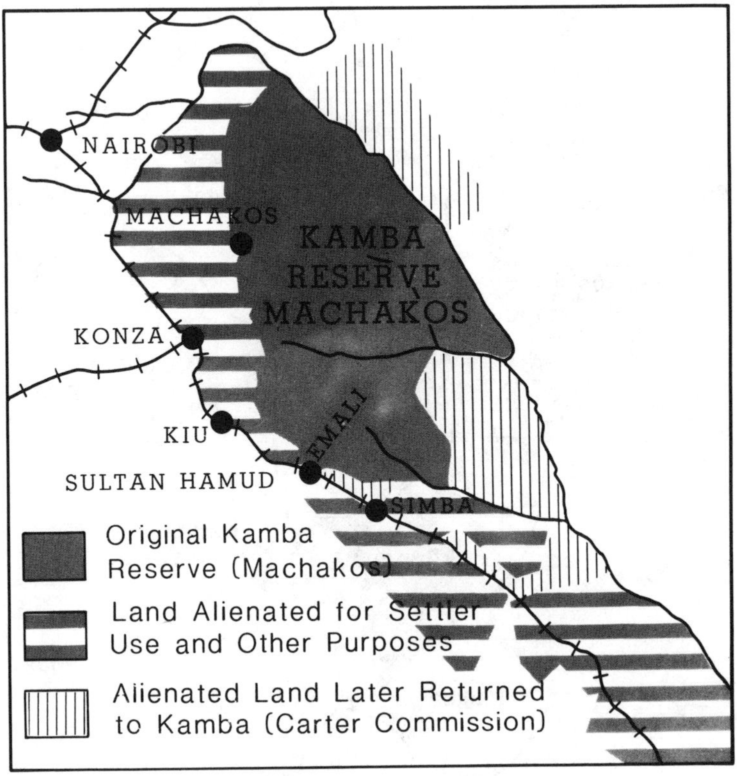

Figure 3.2 The Changing Boundaries of Machkos Kamba Territory

restricted, reducing Kamba pasturage by about fifty percent. Some of this territory was restored to of Machakos District after 1960.

Between 1908 and 1910 the Mua Hills were alienated for European settlement. This decision was justified on the basis that the area was not required by the current Machakos population, yet approximately 2000 Africans had to be resettled to make room for British colonists. According to later surveys, the Mua Hills formed a substantial component of the high potential land available to the Kamba.

The general excuse given for land alienation was the sparse population of the district. This position was based originally on reports of missionaries and travelers during the late 1800s which allude to a paucity of occupants in such areas as Momandu, Kalama, and Matungulu.[6] According to another commentary "areas cultivated were small and much of the wood cut down was replaced naturally."[7]

These observations reflect the limited perspective of the outsider rather than the reality of conditions in Ukambani. To those unfamiliar with the agricultural system and the cycle of cultivation and temporary fallow, the territory available to the Kamba must have seemed adequate; certainly there was little evidence of erosion along slopes or sediment clogging rivers.[8] The impression was artificially reinforced by two factors: 1) population losses and migration during the famine of 1899-1900 caused densities to decline in selected areas, and 2) too many of the evaluations of the population-land balance were taken either in lowland areas or in the frontier zones of both northern and southern Machakos which were still partly occupied by bush and game. The lowlands appeared to be sparsely populated, but they formed an important spillover area for pasturage, hunting, and obtaining firewood and building materials. Certainly the more discerning of observers also mentioned either that it was difficult to estimate population densities since fields were scattered and dwellings often hidden or that some of the hill massifs were fairly thickly populated.[9] One estimate of the population density of the Iveti Hills, for example, was 57.69 persons per square kilometer.[10]

In effect, land alienation was based on an inaccurate view of the existing situation and little concern with the impact of either population growth or precipitation shortfalls on the future territorial needs of the Kamba. Yet, population increases had become evident by the time the first settlers began to arrive. It is difficult to reconstruct precise figures, but relative population can be estimated from the surveys that were taken at irregular intervals beginning in the early 1900s. These population counts, based on some combination of tax register information, numbers of dwelling units, and educated guesses as to the average family size, were almost always below the actual figures. The estimated population of Machakos District gleaned from the political record book and annual reports, rose from 102,000 in 1902 to 130,000 in 1910.

The 1918 survey, taken with somewhat more care, showed a district population of 138,400 and some interesting regional variations in density (Figure 3.3). The hill massifs of Iveti, Kilungu and Mbooni stood out with an average of over 38.46 persons per square kilometer and higher localized densities that were already putting strains on the cultivation system. The relatively empty frontier zones of the north and the south were still apparent although these two zones were already evolving along different lines which reflected their disparate physical qualities (Figure 3.4).[11] The northern locations were recognized by both Kamba migrants and the colonial administration as having promising soil and precipitation characteristics. On the other hand, the southern area was described as marginal, periodically dry, stony with shallow soil, and full of dense, tse-tse infested bush to be painstakingly cleared by future settlers.[12]

The problem of rainfall variability was also manifested dramatically at this time. Severe droughts had accompanied the establishment of the colonial regime in Machakos District and continued to occur with disturbing regularity.[13] When a serious famine in 1909-10 affected many of the same areas that had been exposed to a regional drought ten years before, the following commentary appeared:

> The year was marked by acute scarcity of food around the district owing to a period of bad rains extending back three years (especially in the south). The famine led to a considerable migration within the district to its Northern parts and partial expansion to such regions as Kilimanjaro-Taveta and Kibwezi. Some have returned but the southerly portions of the district are not nearly so thickly populated as formerly.[14]

During this early phase of colonial rule the Kamba were still able to utilize many of their established survival techniques. Food exchanges (trading goats and cattle for grain), consuming wild fruits and roots, and the use of alternative activities were still very important. The famine of 1910-11, however, marks the first occasion when the mobility strategy was definitively limited by the colonial policy of land alienation. When, in 1909, the pasturage in several parts of the district became inadequate, requests were placed with the district administration for relief grazing. It was not until 1911, however, that additional land was finally made available for Kamba cattle.[15] Even before this famine had reached its peak, friction had developed between the Mua Hills settlers and the Iveti Kamba, the latter having crossed the designated boundary of alienated land in search of pasturage and firewood.[16]

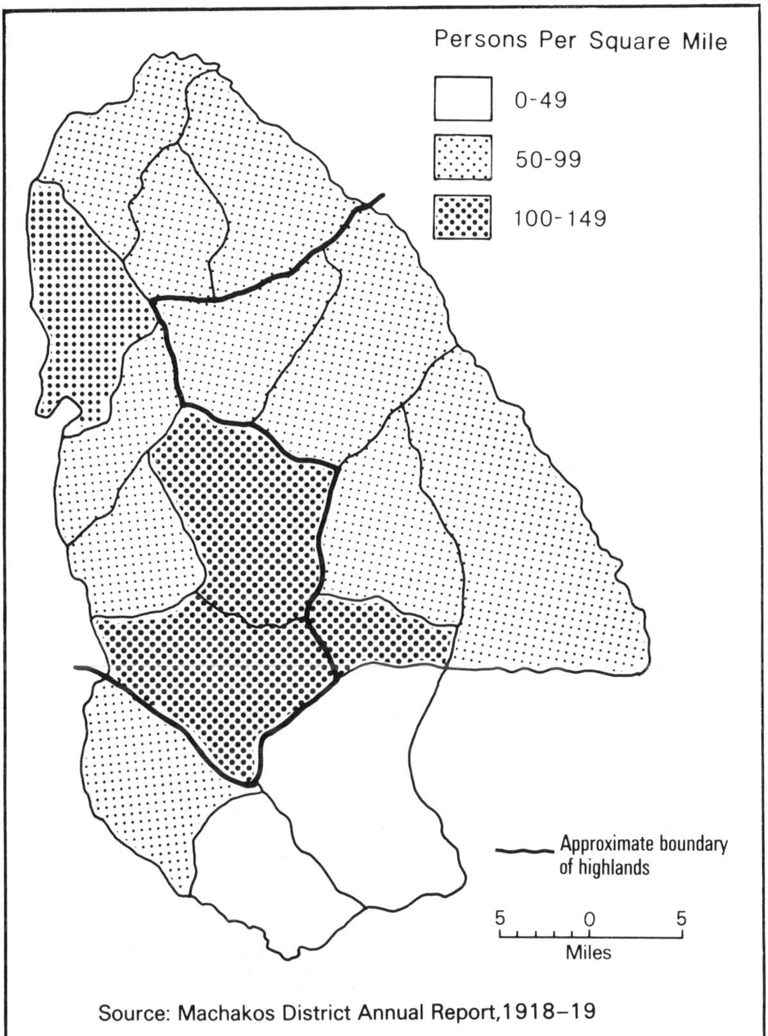

Figure 3.3 Population Density: 1919 Estimates

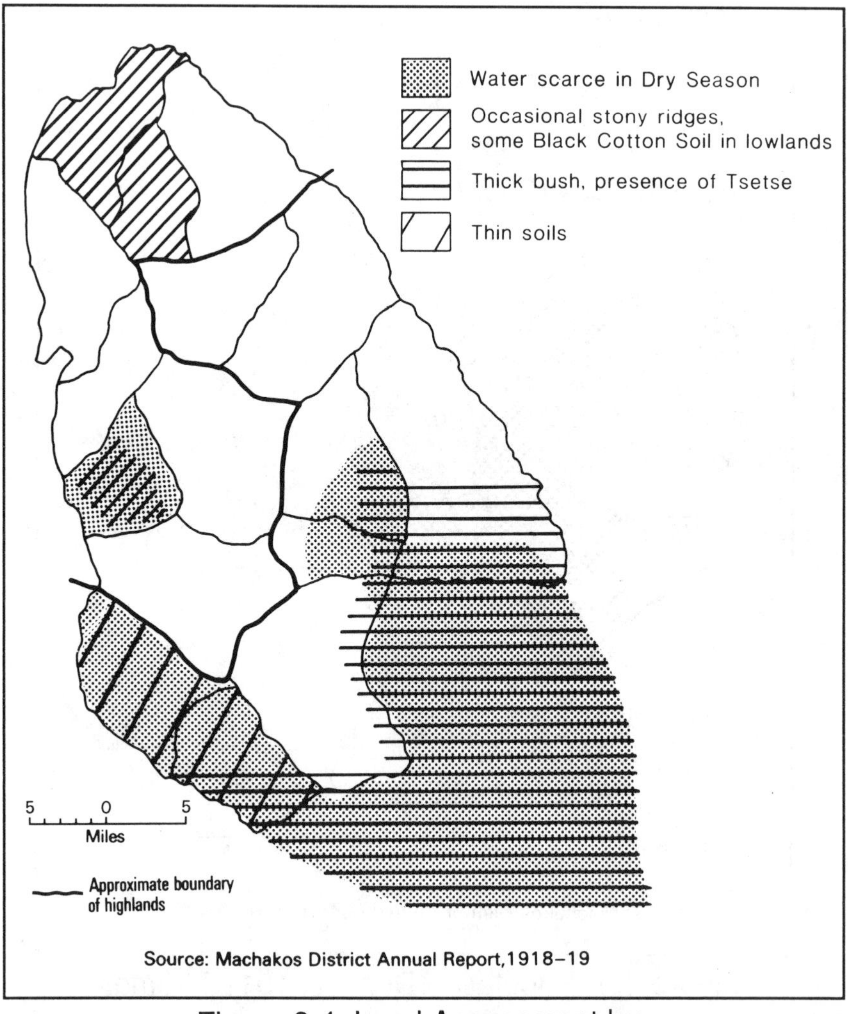

Figure 3.4 Land Assessment by District Officials

Several other contemporary land disputes have been documented. In 1910 the contingent that had been relocated from the Mua Hills to Matungulu were forced to abandon the plots that they had occupied across the reserve boundary. An even more controversial boundary was the western edge of the reserve. This line was repeatedly crossed by Kamba from Kalama, Maputi, Kilungu, and Mukaa, who claimed that the alienated land was a natural spillover zone. A few years later, families who were discovered in prohibited Tsavo territory were collected and returned to their original homes despite protests that their local grain supply was inadequate.[17]

I.B.E.A.C. and later the colonial government also challenged the ritual aspects of the Kamba system of survival by encouraging missionaries to spread an alternative belief system and by desecrating important Ithembo sites. A notorious case of the latter offense took place in 1891 when a large sacred tree was cut down near Machakos town. This provocation led to disturbances which were among the most serious problems of the early I.B.E.A.C. period.[18]

As government officials began to interfere with the Kamba approach to drought, they in turn encouraged the adoption of their own program: the utilization of drought resistant crops combined, in emergencies, with famine relief. They never had the personnel or infrastructure to enforce the first part of their plan so they were forced to rely on the second option. Four famine relief camps were established in 1909-10 but it proved to be impossible to serve the entire district from these sites alone. Thousands of Kamba died before they had could reach the camps.[19]

2. The Colonial Agricultural Policies in Practice

Machakos District had a special importance within Kenya colony as an important source of porters and local supplies until 1899 when the railroad was completed from Mombasa to Nairobi. Since Machakos was located almost twenty miles off the road line, the town lost its entrepot function on the main route into the interior. A road was subsequently built to connect Machakos to the railroad, but it did not reverse the decline of the district into a relative backwater. A report prepared many years later attests to the fact that not much attention was being given to the area since it was felt to be marginal.[20]

Given the colonial administration's limited interest in Machakos District and the dominant role of the settler community, a vigorous economic policy with regard to the African areas would not have been expected. For a short period, however, colonial officials did encourage Africans to upgrade productivity per unit area and engage in cash cropping. The following statement made by an acting provincial commissioner provides the best example of this temporary enthusiasm for African farming:

> One hundred natives, each cultivating five acres (2.2 ha.) of groundnuts, will bring us more revenue than one hundred natives cultivating five hundred acres (202 ha.) for Europeans. They cultivate better for their own economic profit than for a small wage and are more contented in their own environment than as laborers for an estate.[21]

This point of view was opposed by a growing population of European immigrants for whom Africans were more important as wage laborers than as primary producers. The settler community continuously campaigned against government assistance to African farmers, fearing that any improvement in indigenous agricultural methods would provide the Africans with an independent income source.[22]

By the beginning of World War I, it was obvious that the settler community had triumphed in this confrontation. Cash cropping had declined for African farmers as settlers came to control the marketing boards, monopolize the best land, and dominate access to agricultural extension and inputs such as fertilizer and insecticide.[23] In addition, the crop research which took place at experiment stations, limited though it might have been, was all directed to improving European agriculture.[24] The Kamba still exhibited a reluctance to work for Europeans, preferring to earn money for taxes and consumer goods by selling chickens, eggs, goats, cattle or cattle products, bees wax, and gourds. They were sometimes able to find customers among Mua Hills settlers or neighboring Kikuyu, with the Nairobi market absorbing the rest of their products. Yet, for an increasing number of individuals, wage labor became the only source of income.

The colonial administration made only a perfunctory effort in the sphere of African agriculture once the paramountcy of settler interests was established. Initially, the government distributed free seed which was expected to reduce the intensity of famines. Later, cash crops were encouraged, but only those that contributed to the need of the settler community. For example, commercial maize was promoted so that a cheap food supply would be available for employees on European farms.[25] The administration also showed some concern with livestock but it was usually confined to controlling disease and marketing activities or to regulating the number of animals in a given area.

Until the 1920s there were no training centers for African agricultural instructors nor were extension agents posted to African areas. The administrative staff sometimes took on an extension role but their effectiveness was limited by a condescending attitude and by the ability of the Kamba to participate in the cash economy without having to respond to government exhortation. According to one commentary: "the Kamba are not careful about planting maize and beans even when seed was given out because they are rich enough in cattle and able to disregard profits from grain crops."[26]

In essence, the government program which had emerged by 1914 aimed at encouraging two groups within the African population: 1) subsistence food producers who could grow enough surplus for occasional sale and to sustain themselves during a drought, and, 2) potential laborers who would provide the work force on European farms and then return to their homesteads when their services were no longer required.

3. Regional Differentiation

The early colonial period in Machakos also corresponded to the emergence of new regional relationships. At one level, Kenya colony had come to function as a peripheral region within the system of world capitalism while, at a second level, Machakos District existed as a marginal component of Kenya Colony, having lost its pre-eminence after the completion of the railroad. Regional variation could also be discerned within Machakos District itself. At this early stage, the nascent road network played the most important role in determining the spread of the colonial package which combined improved accessibility and marketing opportunities with increased likelihood for Africans to be co-opted into the wage labor system. The more accessible areas corresponded in part to the highlands. Early roads linked Machakos town with Kangundo, Matungulu, Ngoleni (Iveti), Kilungu, and Mbooni, to be sure, but the roads tended to just barely penetrate into the hill massifs proper (Figure 3.5). At the same time, certain lowland areas experienced a higher than expected level of accessibility as a result of their position along the route to Kitui to the east or to the railroad towns of Emali and Simba (Figure 3.2).

The pattern of urban centers which began to emerge in Kenya at this time reflected a complete disdain on the part of the government for any pre-colonial centers of trade or political activity. Instead, in each district, the administration established at least one major center and usually one or more sub-centers, all conveniently sited in terms of access to roads, railroads, or population concentrations. These emerging towns almost always contained housing for the European and African staff, a law court, police station, post office, school, and sometimes a hospital or army depot.[27] In Machakos District, the role of district center was filled by Machakos town. Some divisional headquarters were also recognized although initially they had few services.

At the same time that this urban structure was gradually developing, an overlapping system was being established by church groups. The selection of mission sites was usually based on the same criteria used by the government but the distribution of the cooler highlands was even more important.

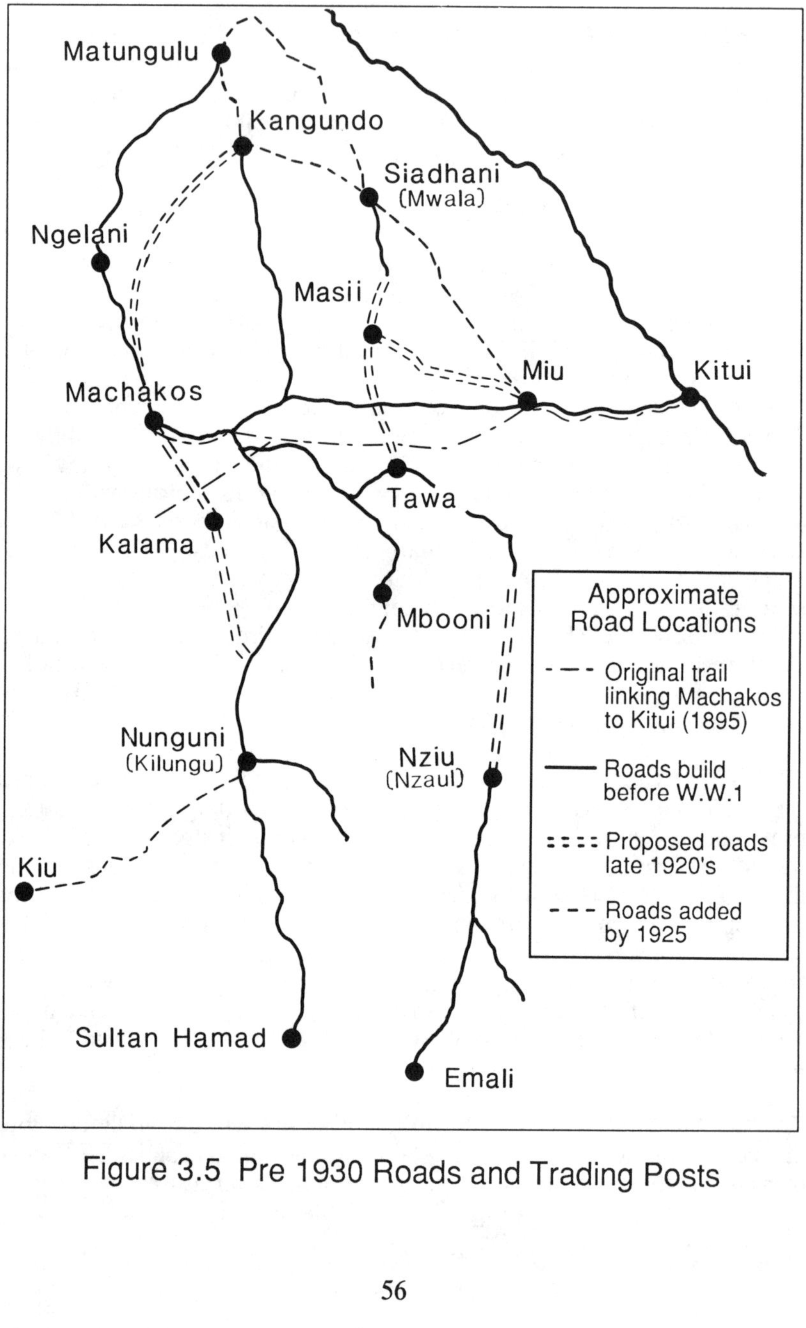

Figure 3.5 Pre 1930 Roads and Trading Posts

These mission stations often expanded to become small urban centers in their own right with schools, dispensaries, related social services or income generating activities.

The important urban function of retail trade came to be distributed more widely. Shops appeared in conjunction with government offices and missions but in addition, they were opened at official government trading posts. The early posts were usually confined to a few shops run by Indian and later African traders but in spite of their limited scope, new posts or shops had to be licensed by the government. Of the five colonial trade centers in existence in 1913 in Machakos District, three were on or near the Machakos-Nzaui-Sultan Hamud road, one was on the road to Kitui, and one was on the road north to Matungulu. All were in the lowlands although four of the five were at least proximate to hill massifs.

The shops and trading centers described above were supplemented by small, scattered periodic markets that usually operated two days a week. The markets were most likely to be found on areas of high agricultural potential or contact zones between different physical/environmental settings. The periodic markets specialized in crops and cattle products in contrast to the shops (known as dukas) which also dispensed some imported manufactured goods.[28] Both markets and shops formed an important link in what was emerging as a very diffuse pattern of distribution for goods and services. In time, the lack of coordination between the elements of the nascent urban system was to create problems and lead to a demand for more centralized urban planning.

In summary, at this early stage in the development of Machakos District, lowlands and highlands continued to be joined by complementary trade and mutual assistance that had been undiminished by economic differentiation. Population movement between the two areas was still occurring in both directions; during years of average rainfall migrants and herders would reach into the more remote lowlands for grazing or cultivation land while during drought periods, movement toward the highlands was predominant. Evidence does begin to emerge at this time of two more permanent and opposing forms of migration: 1) families moving toward Machakos town and near-by hill massifs to share in the perceived advantages of proximity to the focal areas of the colonial establishment and 2) down-slope movement to avoid the initial stage of hillside erosion by overgrazing.[29]

A final overview of the early colonial period in East Africa reveals a government lacking in sensitivity to local issues and unable to adjust programs to the needs of the African population. No effort was made before W.W. I to assess the current or future land requirements of the original occupants of Machakos District, instead wage labor was put forth as an alternative to grazing cattle and farming the land. The authorities reacted with characteristic lack of flexibility when they were faced with rebellion and later civil disobedience over the boundary issues. Instead of designing a policy that would have taken into account all of the relevant factors in the district's mix of people and resources, the administration substituted forced removals of "trespassing" Africans and the encouragement of stock sales. Instead of formulating a coherent approach to the threat of famine they substituted a limited endorsement of drought resistant crops and an inadequate program of famine relief. The crisis that was building up under these circumstances could only be contained temporarily.

CHAPTER 3: REFERENCES

[1] Forbes-Munro, *Colonial Rule and the Kamba*, 29.

[2] Maxon, "John Ainesworth in Kenya," 151.

[3] Goldsmith, *John Ainesworth, Administrator*, 32.

[4] Mariuki, *History of the Kikuyu*, 109.

[5] Forbes-Munro, *Colonial Rule and the Kamba*, 46.

[6] Johnston, *African Inland Mission Report*, 1899.

[7] J. A. Stuart-Watt, *Private Papers*, Rhodes House, Oxford.

[8] Odhiambo, "Rise of the Kenya Peasant," 35.

[9] Ainesworth, "A Journey from Machakos to Kitui," 411.

[10] Gregory, *The Great Rift Valley*. 347.

[11] Oliver and Mathew, *History of East Africa*, 414.

[12] Kenya National Archives, *Annual Report*, 1918-19, 20.

[13] Goldsmith, *John Ainesworth, Administrator*, 46-47.

[14] Kenya National Archives, *Machakos Political Record Book*, 1909-10, 23.

[15] Colonial Office, Kenya Colony, *Machakos District Gazetteer*, 2.

[16] Kenya National Archives, *Machakos Political Record Book*, 1909-10, 23a.

[17] Ibid., 1918-19, 15.

[18] Ibid., 1911-12, 12.

[19] Colonial Office, Kenya Colony, *Papers on Early Machakos History*.

[20] Kenya National Archives, *Annual Report*, 1924, 99.

[21] Ibid., Ukamba Province, 1907-08, 20.

[22] Wolff, *The Economics of Colonialism*, 176.

[23] Leys, *Underdevelopment in Kenya*, 34.

[24] Wolff, *The Economics of Colonialism*, 138.

[25] Van Zwanenberg, *Economic History of Kenya and Uganda*, 49.

[26] Kenya National Archives, *Political Record Book*, 1910-11, 48.

[27] Colonial Office, Republic of Kenya, Ministry for Lands and Settlement, *Human Settlement in Kenya*, 32.

[28] Freeman and Norcliffe, *Rural Enterprise in Kenya*, 33.

[29] Mutiso, "Machakos Political Evolution," 6-8.

CHAPTER 4

THE INTER-WAR PERIOD 1918-1939

1. Agricultural Policy

The end of World War I and the revival of British interest in Kenya had only a limited initial impact on Machakos District. The area finally received an agricultural officer in 1923 but his responsibilities, beyond distributing seeds and organizing a few demonstration farms, were limited to encouraging what proved to be an unsuccessful dam building program.[1] The increase in productivity and adoption of new crops that did occur could be attributed as much to missionaries and agricultural workers returning from settler farms as to any government effort.

When the agricultural officer was transferred as an economy measures the district was left in an even more marginal position. Official reports on the area issued in the 1920s indicate a continuation of the negative attitudes referred to earlier. According to a statement by the acting director of agriculture, the Kamba were a conservative, pastoral people lacking the advantages of the Kikuyu and Nyanza peoples, with little seen for the years of work done by the agricultural department.[2] Shortly thereafter the South African director of irrigation came to the district and advised against the improvement of water supplies primarily because "the Kamba were not skilled in agriculture."[3]

These statements again reflect the uneven impact of marketing boards, extension, and research which provided opportunities in commercial farming only to Europeans. Few Africans were able to take advantage of escalating crop prices in the post war period. The European position was further enhanced by the emerging pattern of infrastructure. Most of Kenya's railroad lines, especially those built after 1920, were designed to serve the settler communities. The emphasis placed on railroad rather than road construction was in itself an indication of settler dominance. The widely scattered African population would have been much better served by a road network.[4]

Pressure on Africans to participate in the labor forces also continued into the 1920s. Recruitment was facilitated first by an ordinance which required the registration of all adult males, then, in 1919, by the release of a circular which called on chiefs and elders to assist in providing labor for European farms. This policy was strengthened by an increase in the poll tax compounded by stricter tax enforcement. All of Kenya colony would have moved inexorably in the direction of forced labor had not mission and other interests intervened to forestall further government involvement in recruitment efforts.

Negative fallout from these activities briefly caused the colonial office to demonstrate an interest in African agriculture but the settlers rapidly regained the initiative in this contest. They achieved, in rapid order, a tariff to protect their production of basic goods (wheat, cheese, etc.) and a ruling that restricted coffee and tea growing licenses to Europeans. Thus, as of 1925 most African farmers still had no cash crop. Their efforts were concentrated on maize which could sometimes be marketed, although most maize was required for home consumption. The exception in this case were the farmers living in northern Machakos District who were able to sell poultry, eggs, fruits and vegetables in the Nairobi market.[5]

This situation was interrupted by the onset of the depression. The economic decline of this period had a dual impact on the conditions which had emerged during the previous decade. On the one hand, prices for basic commodities declined resulting in less income from surplus maize and cattle products and a marked reduction in both wages and the need for Kamba laborers on European farms. Even those laborers who were able to retain their positions found their situation deteriorating as restrictions were placed on the number of cattle they could own and as fewer people were available to divide the required work load.[6] On the other hand, the depression awakened the colonial government to the realization that improved African production might help Kenya's flagging economy. Thus, the government finally became definitively (if not always effectively) involved in African agriculture.

Kamba farmers by the mid 1930s were producing larger amounts of maize and more of it for sale. The expansion of this crop was in part a result of the wider use of the ox plow which allowed the typical cultivator to almost double the acreage that a family could manage in a given year.[7] The increase in maize production was accomplished with very little government assistance. When extension agents were finally introduced, African farmers often ignored their exhortations, regarding the agents as the precursors of unwanted government intervention.[8] This negative reaction was also the result of poor extension advice that was inappropriate given the typical farmer's labor and capital constraints. Agents were not always familiar with the intricacies of local farming systems, and tended to gear their message to the few farmers who were completely integrated into the cash economy.

2. Population and Environment: The Changing Balance

One common problem bound Machakos District together during this period: growing land scarcity due to population increases combined with such manifestations of land deterioration as slope erosion. Between 1918 and 1939 the estimated population of the district went from 138,000 to 241,000. This substantial increase reflected better counting methods as well as an annual population growth rate that sometimes reached 3.2 percent.

The 1939 population estimates also showed greater concentrations in the highlands, especially in the north, while the lowlands exhibited densities of less than 200 persons per square mile (Figure 4.1). These totals are somewhat deceptive as they mask more detailed patterns and fail to convey the precarious nature of the less than 150 per square mile densities in some of the lowland locations. By 1939 it was stated by the district officer that open, unclaimed land, found mainly in Kibaoni, Kaumoni, Nzaui, and Mbitini, amounted to 450,000 to 700,000 acres.[9] This report ignored smaller areas within locations that were either unclaimed or had frequently changed hands, but it did focus on the last obvious frontier where fly and bush still covered numerous tracts. The open areas of the north had disappeared and little land was returned from the alienated sector.

When the first real census was conducted in 1948, it produced the more reliable count of 356,345. By this time some of the highlands had reached densities of over 800 persons per square mile for the first time (Figure 4.2). None of the locations could be considered sparsely populated any longer although at the sub-divisional level small pockets of isolated bush-covered land remained relatively empty.

As early as the mid 1920s the rapid growth of human and cattle populations was leading to land scarcities and land fragmentation. An ancillary factor was the tendency for Europeans and some Africans to increase the size of their holdings in response to the availability of the ox-plow (post-1910) or good prices for cash crops. Whatever the proximate cause, land scarcities were frequently associated with a shortening of the fallow period and a reduction in soil fertility. Studies showed that continuous cultivation resulted in significant declines in crops yields. At the same time, supplies of pasture land were becoming inadequate, a problem that resulted in part from the loss of the active cattle market of the war period. By 1925, the administration was calling for herds to be reduced by twenty to thirty percent. Finally, the exposure of bare soil in overgrazed

Figure 4.1 Population Density: 1939 Estimates

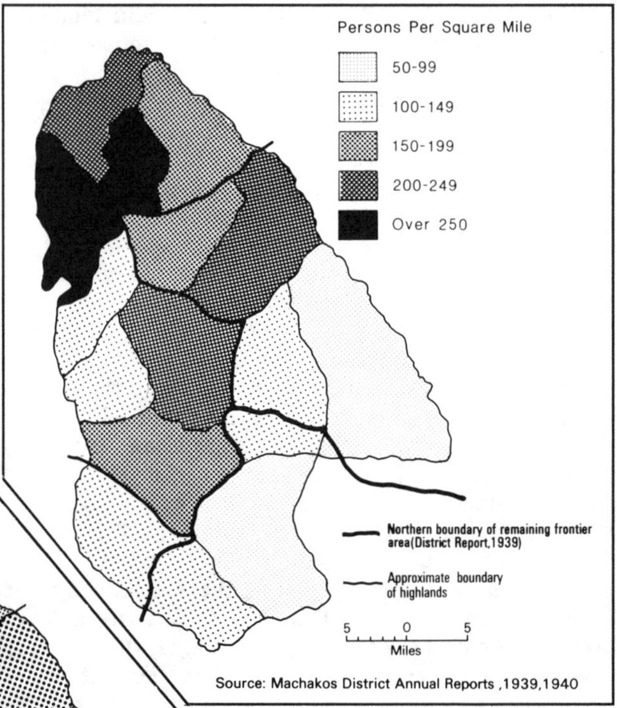

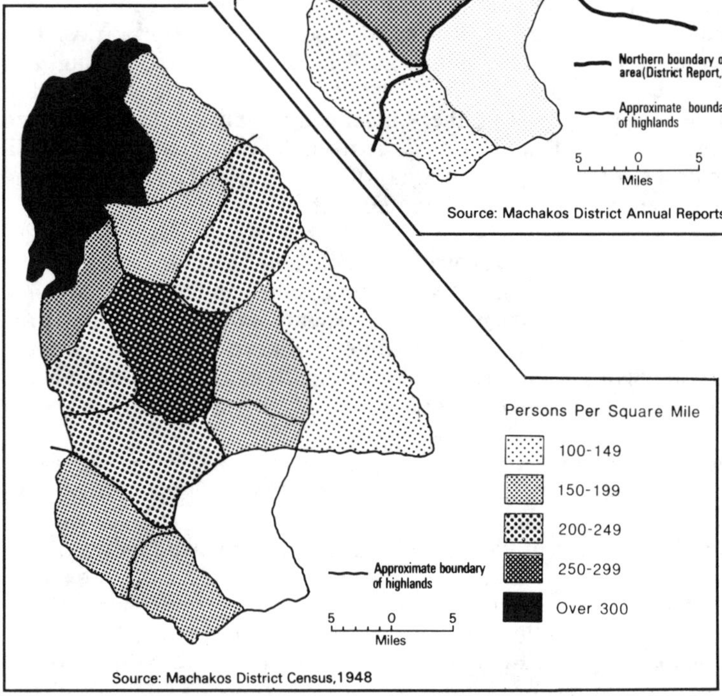

Figure 4.2 Population Density: 1948 Census

areas, combined with the utilization of steep slopes by land-poor farmers, was exacerbating the erosion problem. Loss of top soil implied not only a removal of the soil components that were more fertile in terms of available nutrients, but also a decline in the soil's infiltration capacity.[10] All of these issues were being brought to the government's attention, but little destocking, land consolidation, or rehabilitation could take place at this time due to the limited capacity of the agricultural service and widespread opposition among the Kamba.

By the 1930s, severe droughts and subsequent food shortages had convinced the government that a more coordinated policy was required. Several studies were commissioned including one which emphasized that "the reserve is suffering from severe erosion in various forms with several areas (Matungulu, Maputi) that used to have excellent land for crops rapidly losing cultivatable acres."[11] Estimates of the area affected varied from 40 to 75 percent of the inhabited part of the reserve, with future expansion of deep gulleys said to be inevitable.[12] Whatever the contradictions in the reports, the official point of view was unanimous on one point: the Kamba were ruining their land with "primitive techniques, overstocking and timber cutting," and the antidote was a combination of conservation measures and a more extensive planting of famine-reserve crops.[13] A more realistic assessment would have taken into account the negative impact of the original land alienations and the Kamba attitude toward agriculture and herding.

It was at this time that the Kenya Land Commission was reviewing conditions in the areas that had been reserved for African farming. Although problems of increasing erosion and inadequate grazing land were obvious in the Kamba territory, the Commission members put the blame on the Kamba agricultural system and overgrazing rather than on the loss of half the established area of pasturage to European settlers.[14] They claimed that as many as six cows and six goats might be grazed on a typical four-acre holding (in contrast to the recommended ratio of one head of cattle per ten to thirty acre area).[15]

The Commission ultimately insisted that unless stock numbers were severely reduced, land reconditioning initiated, and yields improved there was no reason to expand the Kamba reserve.[16] It was obvious that the government position was to protect European holdings and economic prerogatives rather than to promote a more equitable land distribution scheme.[17]

While the land question was deftly avoided, several policy lines emerged that were designed to halt the process of soil deterioration: 1) controlled access to eighteen percent of the Yatta Plateau for Kamba herds, 2) selective reconditioning of the reserve, and 3) forced destocking. Reconditioning was initially carried out by a committee that was able, within two years, to have 25,000 acres set aside to be upgraded. One of the side-effects of this process was to accelerate the emergence of individual land tenure since the committee and its successors tended to work with households rather than community authorities.[18] This policy gave further credence to a widespread Kamba belief that reconditioning was intended to improve land for eventual alienation. Gradually, clan control of land distribution was declining at the same time that the old commonage (*weu*) was disappearing.

In addition to grass planting, manuring, and the temporary closure of land to grazing, the reconditioning effort focused on the building of terraces. At one point terracing was to be combined with a program to depopulate selected hillslopes for reforestation, but a more limited tree planting on empty tracts was later substituted. Although widespread terracing was carried out (Table 4.1), it proved difficult to recruit local labor for this effort. This ongoing problem stemmed from widespread resentment of mandatory labor demands and insufficient understanding of the purpose behind terracing. Resistance became more organized with the creation of the Ukamba Members Association, and lack of participation sometimes expanded into outright destruction of completed terraces.

The policy of destocking also aroused negative reactions among the Kamba. The program emerged after much of the damage to the district's grassland had been attributed to excessive numbers of cattle. The administration ignored the fact that the stock supply in Machakos District had not increased more rapidly than the population--in fact, many families had lost stock as a result of famines and a period of compulsory purchase during the war. According to one estimate, cattle needs had not been exceeded by cattle numbers for some time, but the colonial administration still decided to deal with the problem by reducing the cattle population and providing additional grazing land in the Yatta under tightly controlled conditions. Estimates of the dimension of excess stock units by location in 1944 are shown in Table 4.2.

In 1937 there were approximately 250,000 head of cattle in Machakos District, and the administration, through a less than scientific procedure, decreed that there was only room for 100,000.[19] Quotas were established on a community-by-community basis and elders were instructed to decide which cattle would be eliminated.[20] Disenchantment with this procedure was compounded when a new livestock processing plant was established at Athi River in 1937. To the settlers, this was a highly desirable move because such a plant might build a freezing compartment and allow their cattle to enter the world market. To the Kamba, it appeared that the entire program was only a guise for providing the factory with inexpensive raw materials for the production of meat extract, hides, and fertilizer.

Table 4.1

Development of Terracing and Related Conservation Measures
1937-1941

Year	Area Closed to grazing (acres)	Acres of Grass Planted	Area Terraced (acres)	Areas prepared for grass planting
1937	25,000	---	---	---
1938	---	---	304	---
1940	32,810	1,136	---	16,000
1940	16,250	7,978	85,847	---
1941	25,705	3,359	16,740	---
1942	19,320	4,604	13,089	---

Source: District Agricultural Gazetteer, 1958, p. 17.

Table 4.2

Results of Attempts to Estimate Stock Carrying Capacity

Location	Stock Units (Estimate) 1944)	AO estimate of no. of acres needed per stock unit	Max. stock units allowed given area of location	Balance
Iveti	14,800	15	4,352	-10,448
Maputi	2,600	50	589	- 2,011
Kangundo	10,800	15	2,517	- 8,283
Masii	20,000	30	1,493	-18,507
Mwala	26,000	35	2,267	-23,733
Matungulu	14,400	15	2,987	-11,413
Kiteta	10,000	40	1,472	- 8,528
Kisau	26,000	46	1,680	-24,320
Kibani	11,600	50	1,114	-10,486
Kaumoni	2,800	10	1,600	- 1,200
Nzaui	7,000	10	9,024	2,024
Mbitini	11,600	20	2,560	- 9,040
Mukaa	19,800	35	1,865	-17,935
Kilungu	12,400	20	4,288	- 8,112
Mbooni	11,200	30	2,261	- 8,939
Kalama	11,201	30	1,259	- 9,941
	192,200		41,333	

Source: "Machakos Reserve Facts and Figures." (MRFF)

The destocking process began in the north and by July, 1938 about 20,000 head of cattle had been sold in Kangundo and Matungulu.[21] From the beginning, however, the program was complicated by local non-cooperation, subsequent government raids, and numerous incidences of unfair confiscation. Some families with just a few head lost all their cattle while others were able to escape completely into the bush. Finally, over a thousand angry Kamba marched on Government House in Nairobi, an action which resulted in the indefinite postponement of destocking as a conservation measure.

3. The Strategy for Survival

The application of the government's program to problems of land deterioration and famine in Machakos District, once again, ignored the indigenous Kamba approaches to dealing with these problems. The agricultural department staff never bothered to examine in detail the Kamba cropping patterns and related activities, merely labeling them as wasteful and destructive. They distrusted the Kamba capacity to cope with drought and erosion and had only limited expectations for African participation in the commercial economy.

In spite of official disinterest, Kamba strategies continued to operate, although at a reduced scale and in modified form. The most important approach to both drought and land scarcities was relocation, including the practice of squatting. This mechanism involved the exchange of labor on European farms for a small wage and for the right to cultivate food crops and to graze cattle. Squatters were not officially allowed in Machakos District until 1920 due to the questionable administrative position that only undesirables would resettle in the settler areas.[22] Yet, as soon as regulations were revised allowing access to these prime lands, several hundred families moved onto alienated holdings.

Squatting became increasingly important into the early 1920s. By 1926 it is estimated that almost 3,000 adult males and their families were involved and in 1933, four percent of the total African population were thought to be squatters.[23] In the years that followed, however, especially after the depression began, the squatting option became less attractive. Controls were increased at the same time that land for food plots and numbers of cattle allowed per family were reduced. Wages remained low or declined, often amounting to no more than four shillings a month for ten-to-twelve hour days of field work.[24] Employers created further disincentives. They could control crop choices on a worker's plot so as to avoid competition or even limit the time available for laborers to cultivate their own crops.[25] It is likely that a squatter exodus would have taken place at this point if land had still been readily available in the reserve.[26]

Other attempts to use the mobility strategy to deal with drought and population growth were frequently met with frustration. By World War I it has become more common for highland farmers to utilize the lowlands. At first, when some of them advanced with their cattle in search of pasture they reserved a home plot; later they made a more permanent commitment to both arable and pastoral activities in the lowlands. The agricultural methods used by these migrants were extremely extensive, and, in the delicate ecological setting of the lowland areas, land deterioration could set in rapidly. In the early 1920s, the annual reports comment on the depletion of grazing land and the need to drive herds into ever drier areas. During the low rainfall years of 1924-25 many migrant families were forced to move back into the highlands where land was already scarce.

When precipitation conditions improved, cattle were once again driven downslope, but farming remained precarious. Whenever several dry years occurred in succession, water shortages along with the subsequent drying out of pastures would drive people away. Those who stayed behind often had to apply for relief-grazing or graze illegally outside of the reserve. Land for relief-grazing was first sought in the Yatta in 1924 but access was denied and cattle deaths were widespread. For the rest of the 1920s, Yatta grazing was made available for a fee in order to prevent a recurrence of the 1924 disaster. Since no Yatta land was available for cultivation, however, only part of the problem was solved.

During 1928-29, another difficult period, a group of settlers moved all the way to Kikuyuland in spite of regulations to the contrary. The main focus of immigration, the Mwea Plains, did not provide a particularly secure habitat since at least thirty Kamba were later expelled.[27] When, in 1935, the rains again failed in Machakos but were abundant in neighboring districts, several thousand Kamba left for Embu and the coast. The local agricultural staff, trying to avoid territorial conflict, advocated that the Kamba migrants return as soon as conditions improved but realized that compliance was unlikely.[28]

A situation had been reached by the later 1930s whereby many Machakos District farmers were being forced to oscillate between highland and lowland areas with increasing constraints at either end. As land was becoming more of a scarce commodity, permanent cultivation, land registration and sales, tenancy, and for the first time, a landless peasantry emerged as important phenomena within the district. Even when migrants reached out beyond the Machakos area, restrictions might be imposed by neighboring groups or by administrators seeking to prevent confrontations. Under these circumstances, it is not surprising that squatting on European farms or the technically illegal use of alienated land was often necessary to survival.

Other aspects of the traditional Kamba strategy became less significant. Mutual assistance began to decline and the role of the clan and food exchanges between people in the hills and lowlands was reduced in scope. A tradition of cooperation during periods of stress was giving way to associations based on market exchange. As might be expected, in the more remote parts of the district and in neighboring Kitui, it was much more common to aid relatives and friends as well as to subsist on wild products when other food was scarce.

Reliance on supernatural sources of help during droughts continued to diminish and fewer sacrifices were performed. It was reported that many Kamba believed that the Aimu came less often in the wake of European penetration.[29] Missions expanded their influence, sometimes building on or near former places of sacrifice or in areas that had previously been set aside for the Aimu.[30]

Alternative activities continued to be a source of additional income. Kamba traders were recorded in Nairobi and other cities selling goats, in Masailand selling gourds, and in Machakos District selling cattle, bricks, or charcoal. The most important source of income was the sale of labor and large numbers of Kamba, mostly young and male, attempted to earn wages in the cities and commercial farming enterprises of Kenya. By 1933 it was estimated that at least ten percent of the males between fifteen and forty were employed away from home while in some areas the numbers could reach fifty percent.[31] The impact on village life of this type of migrant labor was thus much greater than during the period of hunting and long distance trade.

At this point a major inconsistency could be discerned in the functions and goals of official agricultural policy in Machakos District. The government administrators had come to participate more directly in the ongoing concerns of soil deterioration, land scarcities, and recurrent water shortfalls. Yet, these functionaries had not won the support of the local population. Simultaneously, the administrators' ongoing lack of interest in Kamba practices obviated any chance to incorporate more of the indigenous agricultural system into the district's programs and policies. This stalemate made it difficult to improve the material well being of the rural population or to provide any ready solution to crisis situations.

It was during the following decade that the balance could be seen to shift between the role of the Kamba in coping with drought and related problems and that of the colonial administration. The factors of population growth, the increasing commercialization of agriculture, and the recognition of individual property rights compounded the earlier influence of land alienation. All served to make the Kamba strategies more difficult to apply at the same time that the government came to play a more active role in agricultural improvement, conservation, and famine prevention.

4. Regional Differentiation

It was also during this post-war period that a phenomenon was first recognized that was to endure to the present: the emergence of the Machakos highlands as the favored area and the subsequent neglect of the lowlands. In effect, the highlands received most of the government's attention and thus continued to produce the most impressive results in terms of registered farmers, acres in cash crops, new cash crops cultivated, and highest yields. These areas were perceived as having the best physical conditions, the most responsive entrepreneurs, and being somewhat like Kikuyuland. Yet, the accomplishments of the highland farmers were to a great extent due to the same advantages that had promoted settler agriculture: better marketing facilities and an unequal share of the agricultural inputs available to the district. At the same time, the lowlands, viewed as a problem by the government, fell further behind. The dryer areas were administered through somewhat of a holding action, the negative effects of droughts were minimized but almost no activist policy was pursued that would have improved the commercial status of both livestock keeping and agrarian-based activities.

The emergence of the important highland-lowland dichotomy requires further in-depth examination. One of the factors which contributed to the differentiation was proximity to Machakos town. Market-gardening was first introduced to the nearby area of the Iveti Hills. Later this activity was extended into Matungulu and Kangundo which were able to serve both Machakos and the Nairobi market.[32] Another contributing factor was the concentration of economic incentives in agrarian rather than pastoral activities. It was thus logical that the better watered highlands would be best able to respond to new opportunities. The price of maize nearly doubled during the 1920s while the price of hides actually fell.[33] Cattle prices in the early 1920s to late 1930s fluctuated considerably according to a report from nearby Kitui, but the pattern of a downward trend was definitely established.[34] Furthermore, cattle sales often reached peak-levels at times of drought when prices were likely to be low.

The lowland-upland differences were further intensified by the prejudices of the agricultural administration which show up clearly in the annual and agricultural reports. One of their first attempts to convey the highland concentration of responses to exhortations occurred in 1927 (Figure 4.3a). In 1932, the following statement was made concerning the introduction of new seed as well as improved maize varieties: "Work in the district has concentrated on the more advanced areas but it is hoped to get to the arid areas shortly." The 1934 annual report contained a short overview of

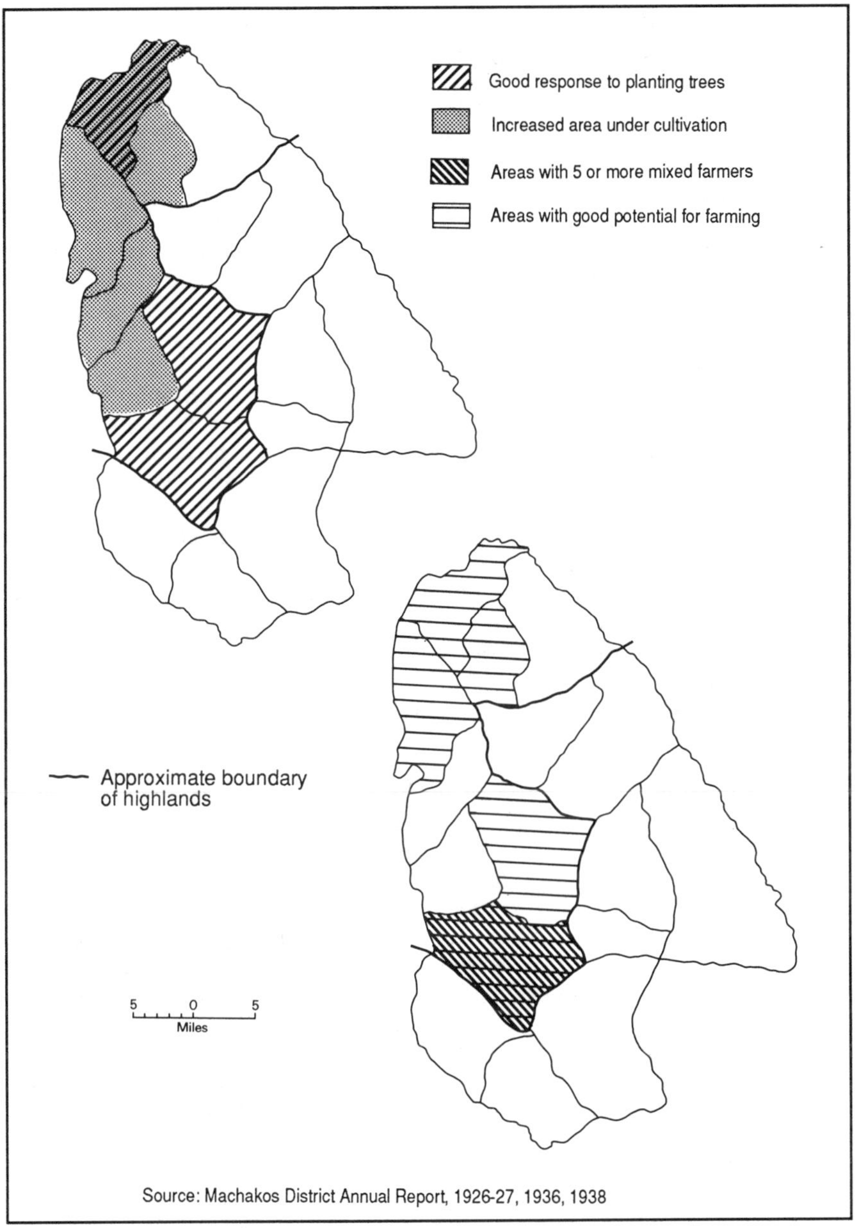

Figure 4.3 The Distribution of Selected Agricultural Department Activities

a drought followed by the remark that increasing progress was being made in Kangundo, Iveti, and Matungulu.

During the mid-1930s, favorable comments were made concerning the cultivation of new crops (onions, wheat, potatoes) and the utilization of ox-carts in the highlands. After several years of campaigning for this type of development, the agricultural office took the position that only selected areas would be worth a heavy investment of personnel for the encouragement of small holder farming (Figure 4.3b). As for the drier areas, there was little expectation of success because of "lower rainfall, unresponsiveness, and the relatively larger holdings that were deemed necessary for each farm unit."[35]

The most emphatic indicator of regional differentiation was the distribution of facilities including those provided by the government and those contributed by missions. As mentioned earlier, the location of missions was most skewed in favor of the highlands. The first missions, other than some abortive efforts by German Protestants, were established in the vicinity of Machakos town. Once these sites were occupied, the next locations to be chosen were in the highlands where an equitable temperature regime, and a presumption of high agricultural potential were combined with a relatively large number of potential converts to Christianity. A few missions were founded just beyond the hill massifs of the edge of the lowlands (Mukaa, for example), but for a long time much of the southern and eastern parts of the district were uninfluenced by either the direct or indirect ramifications of Christian proselytizing.[36]

The missionaries were not particularly successful at attracting converts but they did perform the important function of creating schools, a precedent that was soon followed by the government. Almost all of the bush schools were within or close to the highlands, in part as a response to higher population densities. The government did recognize, however, that lowland children were less well served, even on a per capita basis, than their highland counterparts and some efforts were made to achieve district wide coverage for primary education (Figure 4.4). For example, the government insisted that schools were to be built in such lowland areas as Kibaoni and Kaumoni but, ultimately, there was no real effort to procure the financial assistance needed for this particular plan. As late as 1927, when twenty-one additional bush schools were being designated, the new sites were once again located predominantly in the highlands.

The same arrangement emerged as health facilities were gradually introduced into the region. By 1930 the first "Native hospital" and five dispensaries (known as medical aid outposts) had been opened. The hospital was sited in Machakos town and four of the five dispensaries were located in the highlands (Figure 4.5). Eleven dispensaries were functioning by 1929

Figure 4.4 Government Schools 1900-1926

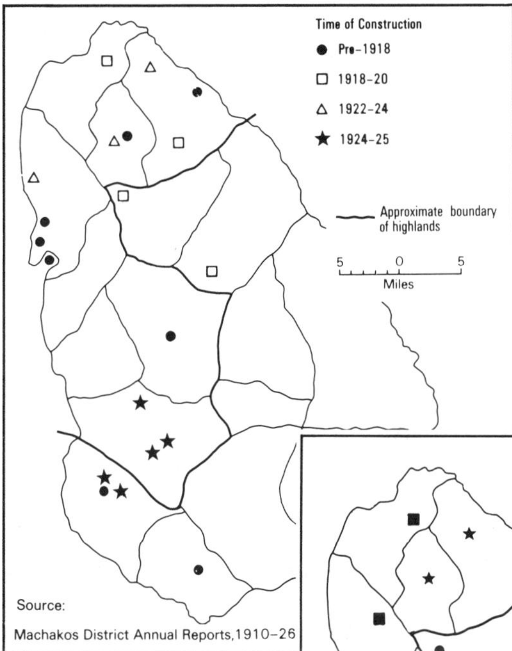

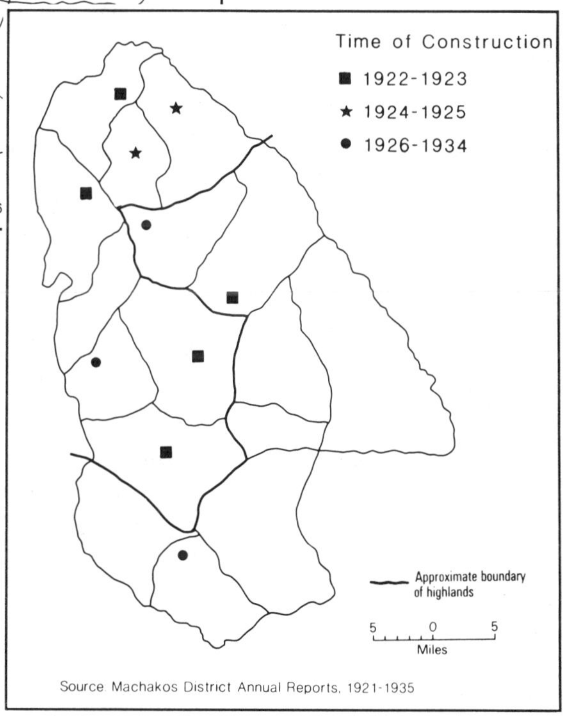

Figure 4.5 Government Dispensaries 1922-1934

but at this point the pace of expansion slowed due to the worsening economic situation in the colony. As of 1935 new openings had balanced closings so that the total number of facilities was still eleven. The distribution continued to reflect a highland orientation even though most of the highlands were relatively accessible to the Machakos hospital while the lowlands tended to be remote from any health service.

Utilization of the hospital increased annually between 1922 (360 inpatients, 3,786 outpatients) and 1932 when the comparable figures were 1,275 and 5,002. In spite of these impressive totals, it could still be said in 1924 that "the hospital is unpopular with Akamba who live in the more remote parts of the district."[37] The term unpopular can be questioned here since evidence at both the hospital and the dispensaries would indicate that the facilities were utilized as long as they could be reached by foot on a one day round-trip journey.

The question of accessibility in turn requires an examination of the growing network of roads and official markets. It would seem from the less than complete evidence of the annual reports and contemporary maps that much road building during the 1920s involved improving existing routes and extending them deeper into the highlands. In 1928 two new major routes were proposed in the Annual Report, an alternative route to the railroad towns that would either skirt or pass through highland areas, and a route connecting three towns and "opening up" the lowland locations of Kaumoni and Kisau. The latter plan represents a rare recorded effort to incorporate remote areas into the district's circulation system. In any event, the austerity of the 1930s slowed down the implementation of these projects and their repetition elsewhere.

The pattern of trade center distribution began to change at this time. Thirteen new centers were opened between 1919 and 1933 and of these nine were either in the center or toward the periphery of highland massifs. The lowland centers of the pre-war period had been widely dispersed along major long distance roads, but new centers built after 1919 were, with one exception, located within ten miles of the highlands.

The combined effect of all of these factors was to create two very different sets of social and economic conditions. In the highlands farmers had been earning cash for some time by growing surplus maize, peas, and beans but by the 1930s the locations of Iveti, Kangundu, and Matungulu had increased their repertoire to include onions, potatoes, strawberries, oranges, and other fruits and vegetables. Mbioni and Kilungu, which were further from urban markets, came to rely on wattle as a major source of revenue. Many oxen were put into use which meant not only that more land could be cleared but also that buildings materials could be hauled out to the fields and crops could be carried to market.[38] The regional economic success was also reflected in the nascent movement toward self-determination; in 1941 a regional official noted that "in the three more advanced areas of Iveti, Kangundo, and Matungulu the political situation bore watching."[39]

At the same time the south and east fell into an increasingly backward role. The problem was recognized by some administrators as evidenced by the following statement: "It is hoped next year to open plots in arid areas which are much in need of early maturing and drought resistant varieties of crops."[40] The only major effort to introduce a new crop, however, was an experiment with cotton planting in the 1930s. Cotton was first grown in Mukaa and Masii, with plans to expand to seven other locations. Some three thousand acres were eventually planted but yields were low in spite of initial enthusiasm for a crop that "provides a useful contract between the government and the more remote parts of the district and without which many farmers will have no cash."[41] The effort was finally abandoned without a sufficiently long trial-period, having been undermined by the use of compulsion, low market prices, pest-problems, and drought. Thereafter, the discouraged agricultural officers concentrated on avoiding famine by encouraging the planting of at least one-half acre of such hardy crops as cassava. An experiment was made in 1939 with the introduction of village industries (weaving, spinning) but this effort was too small in scale to have a substantial impact. Meanwhile, the lowlands remained subsistence based, relatively remote from missions, schools and health facilities, and less involved than the hill massifs in urbanization or participation in the larger economic system.

CHAPTER 4: REFERENCES

[1] Kenya Archives, *Annual Report*, 1924.

[2] Colonial Office, Kenya Colony, R. Harrison, *Efforts to Stimulate Production*, 1924.

[3] Colonial Office, Kenya Colony, *Political Record Book*, 1921-25, 33.

[4] Brett, *Colonialism and Underdevelopment in East Africa*, 200.

[5] Kitching, *Class and Economic Change in Kenya*, 51.

[6] Leys, *Underdevelopment in Kenya*, 47.

[7] Kitching, *Class and Economic Change in Kenya*, 94.

[8] Hyden, *Tanzania After Ujamaa*, 78.

[9] Colonial Office, Kenya Colony, *Machakos Reserve: Facts and Figures*, 36.

[10] Moore, "Land Use and Erosion in Machakos," 424.

[11] Colonial Office, Kenya Colony, *Barnes Report*, 2.

[12] Colonial Office, Kenya Colony, C. Maher, *Soil Erosion and Land Utilization*, 16.

[13] Kenya Archives, *Annual Report*, 1925, 26.

[14] Wisner, "Man-Made Famine in Kenya," 11.

[15] Lynam, "An Analysis of Population Growth," 48.

[16] Kimambo, "Economic History of the Kamba," 90.

[17] Harbeson, "Nationalism in Kenya," 15.

[18] Penwill, *Kamba Customary Law*, 37.

[19] Myrick, "Colonial Initiatives and Kamba Reactions," 9.

[20] Forbes-Munro, *Colonial Rule and the Kamba*, 220.

[21] Myrick, "Colonial Initiatives and Kamba Reactions," 15.

[22] Kenya Archives, *Annual Report*, 1912, 13.

[23] Colonial Office, Kenya Colony. Agricultural Gazetteer, 1953.

[24] Okumu, "Kenya, 1900-1930," 81.

[25] Ibid., 83.

[26] Mbithi and Barnes, *Spontaneous Settlement*, 16.

[27] Forbes-Munro, *Colonial Rule and the Kamba*, 198.

[28] Kenya Archives, *Kenya Native Affairs Report*, 1935, 13.

[29] Mbithi, *New Testament Eschatology*, 135.

[30] Lindblom, *The Akamba of East Africa*, 216.

[31] Lynam, "An Analysis of Population Growth," 44.

[32] Kenya Archives, *Annual Report*, 1926-29.

[33] Van Zwanenberg, "The Development of Peasant Production," 44.

[34] Stanner, "The Kitui Kamba."

[35] Kenya Archives, *Annual Agricultural Report*, 1936, 12.

[36] Forbes-Munro, *Colonial Rule and the Kamba*, 121.

[37] Ibid., 1924, 32.

[38] Forbes-Munro, *Colonial Rule and the Kamba*, 170.

[39] Kenya Archives, *Annual Report*, 1941, 2.

[40] Kenya Archives, *Annual Agricultural Report*, 1932.

[41] Ibid., 1940, 3.

CHAPTER 5

THE EXPANSION OF THE COLONIAL PROGRAM

By the post-war years, Machakos District locational boundaries had evolved to resemble the pattern shown in Figure 5.1. The colonial position on African agricultural development had also evolved to the degree that relative indifference was replaced by two substantial programs designed to improve productivity in the African rural sector. The first of these, the African Land Development Board (ALDEV), was formed between 1944 and 1946 to amplify the theme of land reconditioning and related activities. The second program, known as the Swynnerton Plan when it was finally formalized in 1954, was geared to expanding African cash crop production.

1. The Impact of ALDEV

From its inception, ALDEV dealt with the deteriorating forest, soil, and water resources of the district and their impact on food supplies. These efforts were stimulated by the visit of Mr. Creech-Jones the colonial secretary in 1946. The following account conveys the essence of his reactions:

> He drove mile after mile through hillsides and plains left bare in many places to the solid rock, through areas where there was not a vestige of grass, through acre after acre of dead and wilted maize . . . a fair comparison can be made with parts of British Somaliland--sand rivers lying between bare red hills.[1]

The efforts of the previous decade had obviously been insufficient and moisture shortage combined with increasing numbers of cattle and people were resulting in higher levels of erosion and a more complete destruction of the grass cover. The extent of the precipitation problem can be assessed from Table 5.1, a compilation of qualitative commentary on the regional impact of water shortfalls culled from the agricultural reports between 1925 and 1946. These documents not only indicated the district-wide problem of

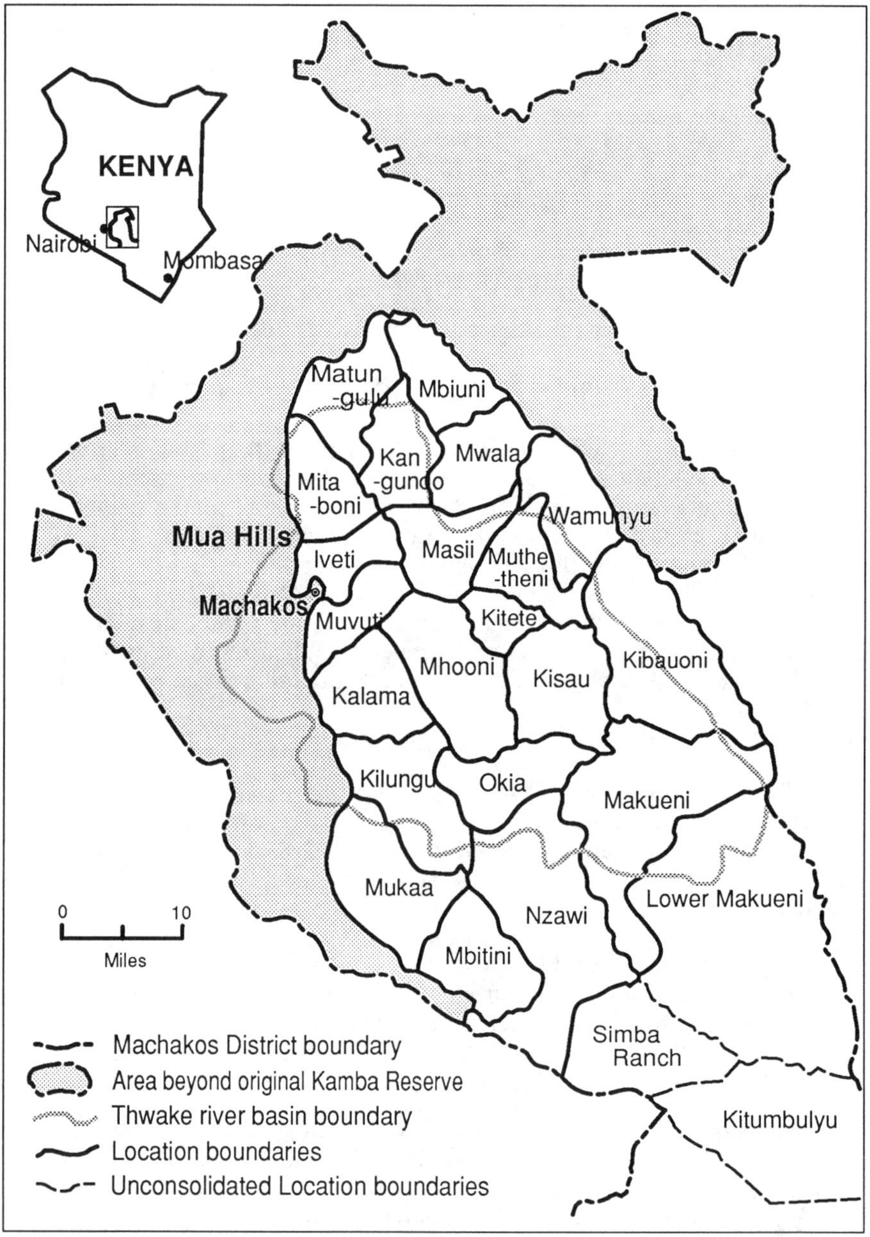

Figure 5.1 Administrative Divisions, Machakos District 1955.

Table 5.1

Descriptions of Precipitation Shortfalls and Subsequent Impact
1925-1946

Year	High Areas	Low Areas	General
1925-2		Exodus of population from worst areas, neighboring areas also reduced to bareness	Drought
1926-27			Mixed
1927-28			Same
1928-29		Many cattle deaths	Long rains poor
1929-30			Mixed
1930-31			Same
1931-32			Drought
1933		Food shortages in many areas, especially Mukaa	Long rains almost total failure, short rains late
1934		Yields poor--especially in Mukaa	Semi-drought--13" below average. With the exception of higher areas the long rains were a failure
1935		Complete failure of short rains in lower areas--Nzaui, Mbitini need increased imports	Semi-drought again
1936	Short rains disappointing harvest down	Short rains below normal normal	Long rains good

Year	High Areas	Low Areas	General
1937		Exceptional to good rains--E. Kiteta, Kisau, Kibauoni	Generally good
1938		Not enough rain in central area	Rains not bad, yields a bit lower
1939		Central area--severe drought again	Acute shortages only millet, beans mature
1940	Rains good in North	Central areas--severe drought again	Rf ceased in middle season--ban on exports
1941			Generally adequate
1942	Exports finally allowed, esp. in Matungulu, Kangundo	Still appears overgrazed in Mukaa, Mbitini	Average
1943	Rains worst in North	Poor in SW & NE Kaumoni, Mbitini did well	Rains not good, crops wilting in March, April
1944		Grazing areas esp. hard hit--only produced 25% of food needs	Drought, RF poorly distributed severe desiccation
1945			Drought continued, food a bit better
1946	Good reports from Kilungu, Kangundo, Mbooni	Crops should he harvested (at least beans and early millets)	Short rains finally well distributed

recurrent failure of the long or short rains, but also pointed to the particular vulnerability of the lowland areas.

Serious food shortages which accompanied these precipitation crises had been occurring on the average of once every three years, and, as of 1943, parts of the lowlands had not been self-sufficient in food for over ten years.[2] Some areas had experienced two to three years without sufficient rainfall, and a consequent lowering of the water table had made it difficult even to use sand wells. In the highlands, where droughts were less severe, the problems of erosion and land scarcity continued to undermine the stability of the agricultural system. As a result of either the small size of plots or of an overcommitment to cash cropping, insufficient land was left for the cattle whose manure might have compensated for the decreasing fallow period.[3]

One ongoing means of dealing with food shortages had been the provision of famine relief. Typically, maize was imported into the district in large quantities as can be seen for the 1940s from Table 5.2. It was the goal of ALDEV to move away from emergency relief measures and substitute self-sustaining mechanisms which would ensure an ongoing supply of foodstuffs for the district. With this end in mind, famine relief plots had been established in selected areas by 1946, and they continued to be encouraged. Cassava, rapidly maturing millets, and seed potatoes were distributed, but since insufficient personnel were available to ensure that these crops were planted, the recommended one-fourth of an acre plot was often abandoned at the end of a period of food shortage.

The need for famine relief plots was exacerbated by the long-term decline in the acreage of sorghum and millet, the traditional drought resistant crops, as maize became increasingly popular in the district. The changeover reflected the greater labor demands of millet (a crop which requires protection against birds during the maturing stage) as well as its poor yields and market price when compared with maize. Although attempts were made to halt the decline of millet acreage, the process had advanced so far by the 1940s that it became official policy to develop a rapidly maturing maize variety.

Another important ALDEV activity was the encouragement of soil conservation by groups rather than on an individual basis as had been done earlier. Teams were organized, each of which usually corresponded to traditional clan or location based *utui*. The accomplishments of these groups, known as *Mwethya*, were impressive considering they used hand tools with only the occasional assistance of a mechanical unit. The most intensive version of these efforts was carried out in a plot designated as the Makaveti Square Mile. This project was based on the usual grass planting and terracing (Plate 1), but in addition, came to include the temporary closure

Table 5.2

Maize Imports and Famine Relief, 1939-1950

Year	Import-export situation	MM RF-Machakos Town	
1939	Large quantities imported	560.8 mm	(22.08")
1940	Crop exports prohibited	735.3	(28.95")
1941	Shortages in certain lowland areas	1073.2	(42.25")
1942	20,000 bags exported	926.8	(36.49")
1943	Very bad year--62,464 bags of maize imported as well as considerable cassava, cereals and pulses-avr. imports 40 tons a day	530.0	(20.87)
1944	Drought plus locust infestation continues. 234,739 bags of relief food imported-avr. 60 tons a day	874.3	(34.42")
1945	Famine relief all year--188,000 bags of relief food imported	484.3	(19.09")
1946	Rainfall situation improves. 247, 983 bags of relief food imported to compensate for previous shortfalls	689.1	(27.13")
1947	Early imports (31,558) followed by exports after March	1240.3	(48.83")
1948	Some exports early in year later terminated	938.8	(36.96")
1949	Both rains failed, 81,823 bags of maize imported, 10,000 of other cereals and pulses	616.2	(24.26")
1950	Severe drought, 226,793 bags of maize imported, 14,911 bags of grain and pulses	653.8	(25.74")

Source: Peberdy, p. 82

of land to cattle, the subsequent feeding of cattle from household food supplies, the collecting of manure, and the use of only carefully designated routes to bring cattle to water. These techniques led to the restoration of a piece of badly eroded land, but the high concentration of personnel and funds at Makaveti made it difficult to replicate the situation elsewhere).[4]

The building of dams was another line of defense against drought (Plate 2). Much of the initial construction took place in the lowlands utilizing both day laborers who were recruited in exchange for famine relief and a supplemental mechanical unit. Highland dams were built as well, which not only secured a water supply during dry periods but also encouraged irrigation. Unfortunately, it was not long before problems of poor construction or maintenance began to undermine enthusiasm for this strategy. By 1949 some of the older sites had fallen into disrepair and spillways that had become overgrazed and gullied were being used as cattle paths. Some dams were actually destroyed by rain while others were silted up.[5] Those dams which remained functional, however, interjected a new measure of security into some remote and famine prone areas.

The final ALDEV program was the establishment of settlement schemes as a means of relieving overcrowded areas and providing land for unemployed urbanites. The first area set aside for this purpose, south of Kibaoni, was considered marginal but capable of reasonable levels of production with appropriate agricultural methods.[6] It was an area that had once been inhabited by the Kamba before being alienated and had since been allowed to revert to bush.

The principal scheme, Makueni, was originally slated to cover 280,000 acres and support several thousand families on large holdings.[7] The higher land was to be used for rainfed agriculture while the lower, dryer zone would be oriented to grazing. Water was to be provided by a combination of dams, boreholes, and shallow wells. Unfortunately, Makueni experienced many of the problems that characterized other contemporary Kenyan resettlement efforts: cost overruns, a dearth of suitable cash crops, a less than ideal settler population, and inadequate or inappropriate personnel. One of the goals of the scheme was to establish production systems that would be appropriate in neighboring areas where migrants were moving in from the highlands and in this regard Makueni had some success.[8]

The first serious bush clearing and preparation of plots took place after 1945. The initial plans for large holdings (8 to 12 ha, 20-30 acres) had to be modified as it proved impossible for the early settlers to control bush regeneration.[9] As the cost of establishing a family at Makueni decreased from £632 to £149, the enterprise became more viable. Settlers trickled in slowly at first, some mistrustful of the enterprise, but over a thousand settlers resided in Makueni by 1955.[10] As of 1960, 2,500 settlers had joined even

PLATE 1. Terraces in the Kilungu Hills

PLATE 2. Kimutwa Dam: A Concrete Structure Built along a Spring-fed Stream

though the income goal of £70 per family plus subsistence was never reached and water conservation problems remained.

Other small scale schemes were introduced during the ALDEV period but these differed in scope from Makueni. One of the more important was the opening of 97,128 ha (240,000 acres) of the Yatta region to grazing. The scheme made use of licenses, fees, and careful water control, but even these regulations did not prevent some symptoms of overgrazing from appearing within a few years.

When evaluating the many features of ALDEV in retrospect, the program can be credited for its technical accomplishments to include substantial terracing, reforestation of some of the steeply sloping land, and improvement of water supplies. Yet, the program was never fully accepted by its alleged beneficiaries whose attitude toward the agricultural department had already been affected by unpopular aspects of the extension effort during the pre-ALDEV period. This negative predisposition was then compounded by the strategies followed by ALDEV itself which were based on a combination of persuasion and forced participation. Farmers were initially encouraged to make group efforts to build terraces or dams, but if their work effort was considered insufficient, local officials might stipulate a required amount of labor over a given time interval. Gradually, interest in terrace building or grass planting tapered off from the peak year of 1958, when 41,684 ha. (103,000 acres) were subjected to conservation measures.

Active opposition to ALDEV was at first sporadic,but it later became more clearly defined with the widespread rejection of large scale reconditioning. Although few concerted group efforts took place that were comparable to the earlier march on Nairobi, the long term commitment of Machakos District farmers to conservation was undermined.[11]

2. The Impact of the Swynnerton Plan

The government itself began to lose interest in ALDEV-type measures by the late 1950s as a result of both lessening local cooperation and the growing influence of the Swynnerton Plan. Critics of ALDEV had complained up to this time that the program had encouraged the continuation of wage labor, traditional tenure, and subsistence crops, in effect perpetuating settler control of the commercial sector. The Swynnerton approach, in contrast, sought belatedly to provide improved commercial opportunities for African farmers through the upgrading of markets and infrastructure, the delivery of needed inputs, and the gradual consolidation and enclosure of land holdings. The motivation for these new efforts was in part the Mau Mau confrontation and other political movements that gave strong evidence of African dissatisfaction with the colonial regime. The government decided to buy time by providing selected farmers with the option of investment and profit.

The Swynnerton Plan contributed to the further differentiation of highland and lowland Machakos. When sites were required for experiments, it was the highlands that were deemed most suitable for this purpose (Figure 5.2). Both the prejudices of the agricultural staff on this issue and the results of the unequal distribution of resources during earlier decades continued to show up clearly in the agricultural reports. During 1951 there were discussions concerning possible coffee production in some of the progressive areas which were defined as the highlands along with Mukaa and Masii (Figure 5.3). The north and west were also identified as having the best diet, showing the most initiative in small scale irrigation schemes, and making the greatest efforts at terracing. Similarly, the completion of roofed cattle compounds was expected to be most successful in the highland locations of Kangundo and Matungulu.[12] The people of the northern divisions were said to be "clamoring for assistance," so as to be able to take advantage of any new opportunities.[13]

Given higher levels of government commitment, and an established commercial base, the highlands moved more definitively into cash crop production in the 1950s. The restrictions which had prevented African farmers from growing selected cash crops were finally lifted, in spite of an ongoing reluctance and fear of competition on the part of the settler community. The most important of these formerly restricted crops was coffee. It was first grown in Kangundo and Matungulu where high standards of cultivation were maintained by farmers who had often learned about the crop as laborers for Europeans. Regulations were introduced to allow production only in specified areas, but the profitable crop was surreptitiously extended beyond this zone, also with good results (Table 5.3). Higher on the slopes, above the areas best suited to coffee, the peasants of Iveti, Mbooni, Kalungu and Matungulu continued to expand wattle production.[14]

Coinciding with coffee expansion was the increasing importance of fruits and vegetables. Rain-fed tomatoes, onions, cabbages, and cow peas were widely dispersed through the northern locations and Mbooni, as were such fruits as citrus, strawberries, peaches, apricots, plums, and mangoes. Since the rain-fed vegetables had considerable competition at the markets in Nairobi and Thika, an irrigation program was initiated in the Kyuu Valley, Mbooni that successfully produced off-season vegetables.

At the same time that the highlands were adapting to an increasingly commercial agricultural economy, the larger farmers within the area were receiving a disproportionate share of locally available inputs and expertise. It was during the 1950s that a distinct class of relatively wealthy African farmers emerged, a social fissure comparable to the spatial hierarchy that

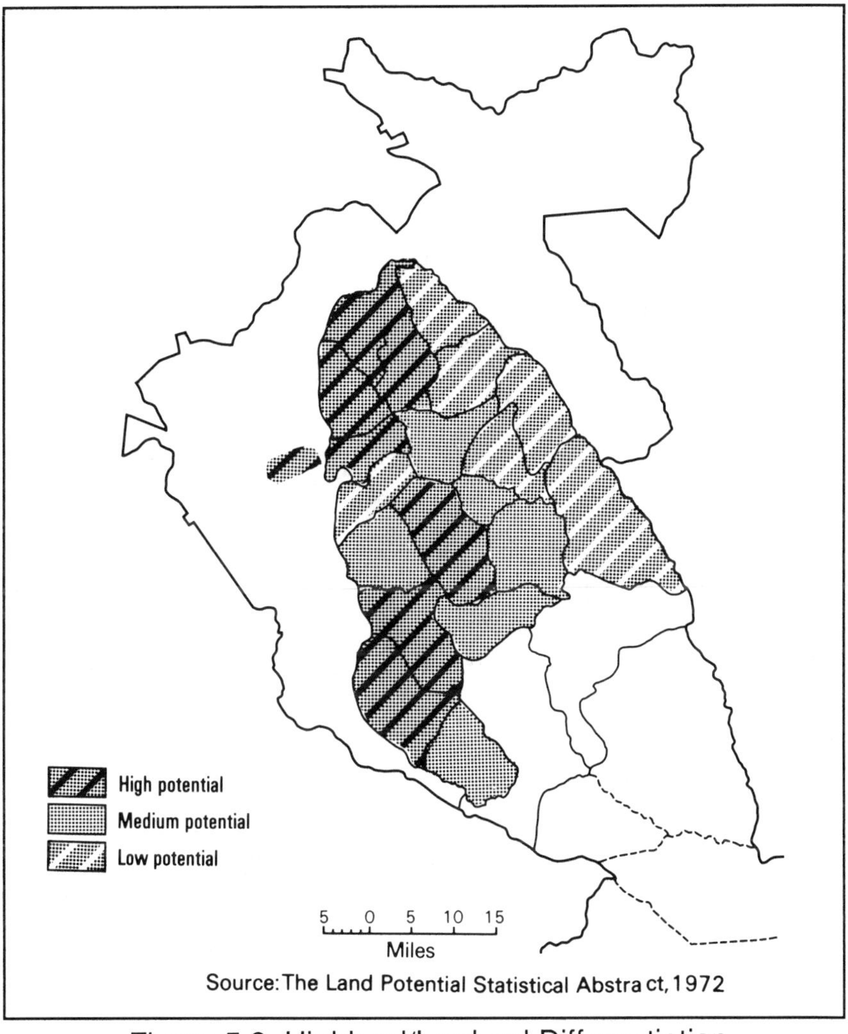

Figure 5.2 Highland/Lowland Differentiation by Land Potential Analysis

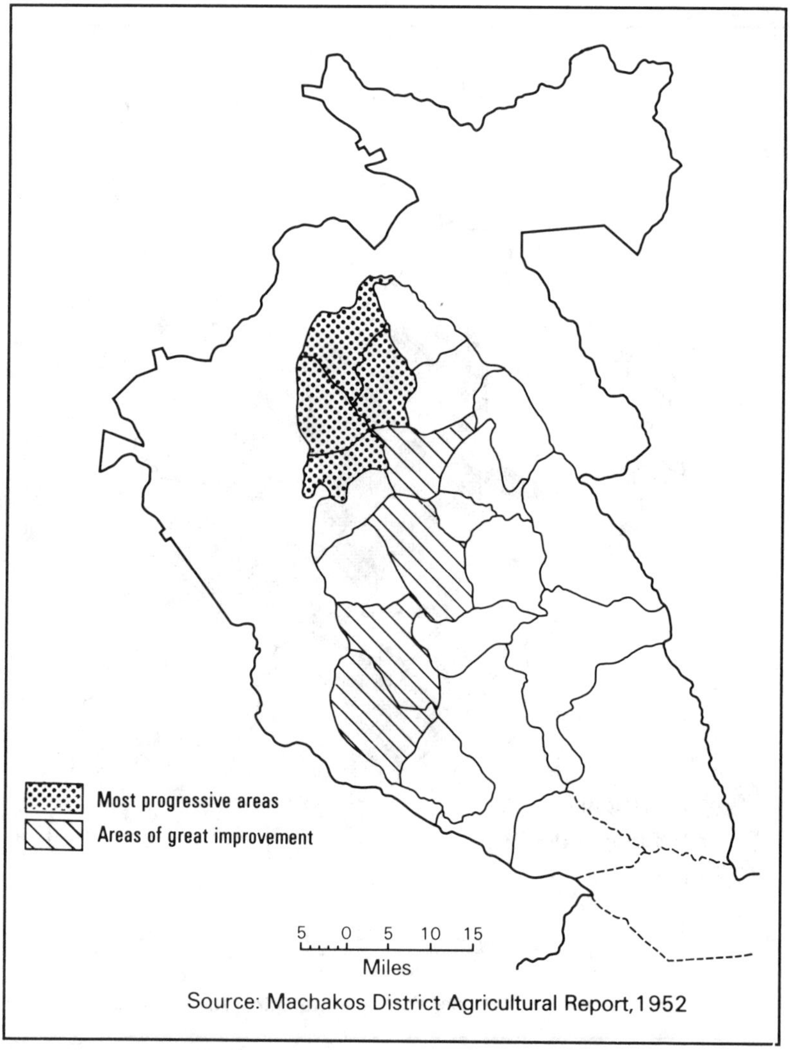

Figure 5.3 Assessment of Progress in Agriculture by Location

Table 5.3

Expansion of Coffee Production

Society: Initial Name	Subsequent Name	Approximate Number of Growers 1954	1958	1964	1972
Kangundo	Muisoni	211	894	2590	838
	Mbilini			1526	
Kikima (Mbooni)		349	1057	1418	
Mitaboni		2	15	1327	905
Iveti		Neg	111	2129	2785
Kilungu	Kithangathini	6	52	2460	1462
Mukaa	Kilalani	2	22	484	875
Muputi			2	310	288
Mbitini	Kithumani			539	220
Kituii (Kangundo)				970	907
Kakuyuni (Kangundo)				1685	758
Matungulu		110	399	(4087)	4232

Source: District Agricultural Reports

had already developed. Many of these individuals resembled their settler counterparts in that they had clear title to their land, had acquired managerial skills, and depended extensively on hired labor.[15] The prosperous minority availed themselves of better education opportunities for their children, as much assistance as was needed from agricultural advisors, and considerable credit. They were also grouped into better farmers clubs and asked to participate in classes at farmers' training centers. Their existence reflected one of the basic objectives of the Swynnerton Plan: "to devote personal attention to individuals who were exhibiting progressive tendencies and, in turn, to create a group of yeoman farmers who would provide a stabilizing force in the rural areas.[16]

The larger-scale farmers also benefited from the design of extension programs. Techniques were introduced that were more appropriate for enterprises based on mechanization or hired labor than for those utilizing only family labor. Similarly, more attention was paid to cash crops than food crops and to the problems of pure-stand rather than mixed-stand cultivation. There was also a special relationship between most extension agents and the prosperous farmers which allowed the latter to be selective in accepting suggestions. The average cultivator, on the other hand, was intimidated, manipulated or misled by extension agents. The mass of the peasantry continued to exhibit toward the extension staff an attitude that ranged from indifference through suspicion to actual hostility.

Thus, the policy of encouraging selected farmers to enrich themselves brought about a polarization within what had been a fairly egalitarian society. It created differences in income and opportunity that could only be exacerbated by population growth and increasing commercialization.[17] Gradually, a fluid situation in which farmers could expand their acreage or in other ways move into cash-crop marketing was changing into a more inflexible system that allocated inputs to a narrowly defined segment of the peasantry.

The lowlands during the post war period were still considered barely suitable for the expansion of commercial agriculture. The area was described as primarily subsistence oriented, with a population that was apathetic and backward because "no future is seen in the industrious working of the land which seems unable to give them a living."[18] A subsequent report was equally pessimistic proclaiming that "the more arid locations toward the east and south bounded by the Athi River and Makueni are backward and impoverished with land seriously deteriorating . . . it will be many years before any advances in farming are seen."[19] As late as 1959 it was still being said that "within the rainbelt agricultural practices are improving rapidly but outside these areas the standards continue to be regrettably low."[20]

As a result of this attitude, only a few cash crops were introduced at lower elevations. An effort was made to investigate the commercial potential of fruits and vegetables that were already being grown in valley bottoms, but it was decided that marketing problems, due either to isolation or lack of organization, precluded any expansion of production. In the late 1940s tobacco cultivation was attempted at Makueni settlement scheme but the project was soon abandoned. Local fuel supplies were inadequate, and levels of production could not be brought high enough to maintain staff and marketing facilities.[21] The District Council then encouraged sisal as an appropriate lowland crop and some success was experienced between 1946 and 1952. The potential popularity of sisal was reduced, however, by the five years required for its maturation and by an unstable market situation.[22] Production did not cease completely after a rapid fall in prices during the mid-1950s, but remained instead at a relatively low level for the purpose of providing boundary markers and such by-products as rope and woven mats.

A further deterrent to crop expansion in the lowlands was a scarcity of adequate land. Although population densities were considerably in the highlands (Figure 5.4), some lowland areas were in pasture that local inhabitants were reluctant to plow up while others were in thick bush that was difficult to clear. In effect, pastoral activities appeared to offer the best promise of a cash income in the lowlands although much more livestock control and related measures would have been required to better exploit the commercial potential of this resource. Dairying was proposed as an option at one point but the familiar problems of erratic rainfall as well as the question of disease control put an end to this line of speculation. As a result of the limited sources of income available to lowland farmers, the economic differentiation of the highlands did not penetrate the southern and eastern portions of the district at this time. It was not yet obvious that the livestock industry, still relatively disorganized, would become a source of wealth to the few herders who would be able to acquire enough land to establish cattle ranches.

Although a high level of regional economic differentiation was actively encouraged by the Machakos administration, the post-war period was marked by one critical policy change: the government became determined to improve the availability of services in remote areas. This concern for equity of access to services can probably be traced to the same motives that led to the Swynnerton Plan: a fear of growing African resistance to colonial rule. The government also became concerned for the first time with the creation or augmentation of locational centers. These centers were to be chosen by the area council to correspond with either a centralized and accessible site or an established focus of activity within each location.[23] It was hoped that activities and services would gravitate to these centers rather than being scattered among several sites, but little was done to implement this policy until spatial planning was introduced after independence.

Figure 5.4 Population Density: 1962 Census

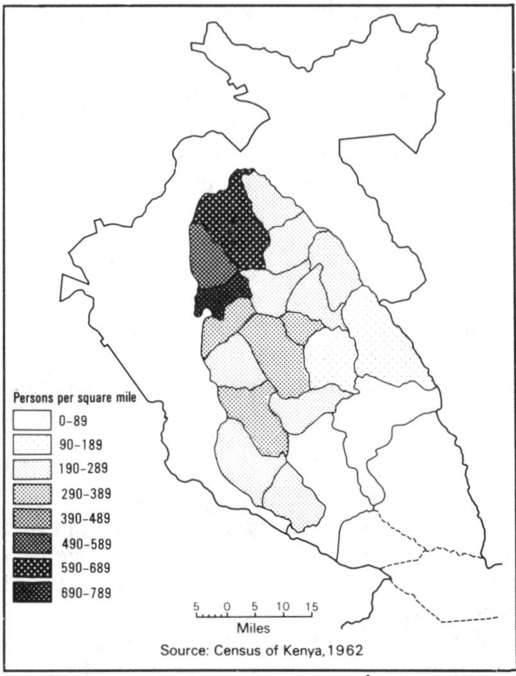

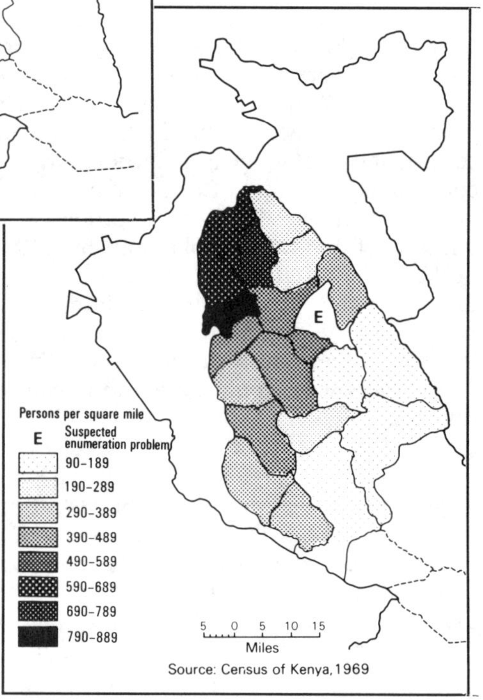

Figure 5.5 Population Density: 1969 Census

Services were most dramatically improved in the sphere of education. The initial plans were particularly ambitious; 23 new primary schools and 4 new intermediate schools were to be built each year from 1952 to 1956. Furthermore, those responsible for siting new facilities were to be particularly sensitive to the location factor. After an education officer reported in 1952 that "there were too many schools in the western locations and too few in the east," locational sub-committees were formed to assist the regional administration in evaluating primary school needs in each area.[24]

By the mid 1950's school construction was close to being on schedule, and government schools were being supplemented by a mission-based school construction project. The distributional programs had run into problems, however, since enrollment in primary schools in the east and south lagged behind expectations and an insufficient number of students were generated to fill positions at intermediate schools.[25] This lack of immediate response to new educational opportunities derived from both the reluctance of parents to lose their children's economic contribution and from the relatively small population within easy access to the new facilities in areas of low population density or poor transport.

Government primary schools had become more equitably distributed on per capita basis if not on a unit area basis by 1955 (Table 5.4). Intermediate schools were less widely distributed and there were still none available in some locations. Adult education programs were also initiated at this time. They were usually organized by locational councils except in low density areas where groups of adults made arrangements directly with individual teachers. The classes were first concentrated in the highlands but by the third year of operation the program had become widely dispersed throughout the district.[26]

Health facilities were expanded between 1946 and 1956 and extended into new territory. Four of the five dispensaries that were opened during this period were located in the lowlands and for the first time health services became available in Mbitini, Kibaoni, and Kaumoni. Attendance at dispensaries in remote areas was initially low (Table 5.5). This phenomenon was the result of the transport and density situation mentioned earlier in connection with school attendance but it also reflected the remote rural population's ongoing reliance on traditional healers. The lowland dispensaries also attracted fewer patients because they tended to have less equipment, medicine, and qualified staff than their longer established counterparts and their fees were often unaffordable to local subsistence farmers. By the mid 1950's the government had reacted to low facility use by curtailing the building of new dispensaries and improving those already in existence.

Table 5.4

Distribution of Primary and Intermediate Schools: 1955

Location	No. Government Primary Schools	Intermediate Schools	Estimated Population 1957	People per* Government Primary School
Highlands				
Iveti	10	3	54,167	5417
Mitaboni	10	2	29,132	3913
Kangundo	16	4	26,505	1651
Matungulu	11	3	25,248	2295
Kilungu	26	3	38,589	1404
Mbooni	12	2	32,600	2722
Intermediate Areas				
Mukaa	19	2	23,114	1217
Kalama	10	1	15,949	1595
Maputi	10	-	7,204	720
Masii	7	1	15,632	2233
Mwala	7	1	28,230	4032
Mbioni	7	1	12,686	1812
Kitete	8	1	25,683	3210
Lowlands				
Mbitini	10	1	15,269	1526
Wamunyu	5	1	18,261	3652
Nzaui	8	1	19,092	2386
Kisau	7	-	22,807	3258
Kibaoni	5	-	14,806	2961
Makueni	4	1	Not available	--

Source: Annual Reports

* Does not include mission schools

Table 5.5

Dispensary Attendance: 1956

Dispensary (Those founded after 1940 have opening date in parenthesis)	Total Patients 1956	Daily Average 1956	Closed by 1962 (X)
(H)* Kilungu	9407	26	X–replaced by regional health center–Nunguni
(H) Nziu (Nzaui)	8678	24	open
(L) Mwanyani (Mbitini)	8833	24	X
(H) Mbooni	7475	20	replaced by regional center
(H) Matungulu	7001	19	open
(L) Tawa (Kiteta)	6723	18	open
(L) Kasikeu (Mukaa)	6048	16	open
(L) Kilala (Kaumoni) (1952)	4535	13	X
(L) Kaani (Muvuti) (1947)	4294	11	X
(L) Miu (Kiteta)	4088	11	X
(L) Upete (Mukaa)	2969	8	X
(L) Mwala	2163	6	open
(L) Katulani (Kibauoni) (1949)	2047	5	open
(L) Okia (1948)	2016	5	open
(H) Kyongala (Kalama)	Not available		open

Hospitals

(H) Machakos town
(H) Kangundo

Regional Health Centers

(H) Nunguni (Kilungu)
(H) Mbooni
(L) Masii
(L) Makueni (settlement scheme)

*(H) Highlands
(L) Lowlands

Another part of the district's program to improve health coverage was the development of a hierarchy of facilities. The central Machakos Hospital was supplemented by a second hospital in Kangundo and a third in Makindu on the rail line. The hospitals were in turn associated with intermediate level health centers which represented the expansion of the dispensaries at Makueni (settlement scheme), Mbooni, Nunguni (Kilungu) and Masii. In each case, improvements were made in the quality of the staff, inpatient facilities were introduced, and, most important, vehicles were made available which would allow access to outlying locations. In 1960, for example, the Mbooni Health Center staff was holding clinics at the dispensaries in Tawa, Miu, and Katulani. Regular visits to nearby dispensaries were also made by doctors and nurses stationed at the hospitals. This approach proved to be effective when resources were adequate (shortages of funds for staff and vehicle breakdowns were not unusual) and demands for new centers frequently emanated from such locations as Mukaa.[27]

By the late 1950s, the regional administration had decided that budget deficits necessitated the closing of several dispensaries. Some low-attendance facilities were allowed to remain open when they provided the only health care available in an isolated area, but the six closings that did take place represented a definite hardship (Table 5.5). The government also encouraged the missions to fill in some of the gaps in the health service system. Although most missions remained highland oriented in the 1950s, they did contribute facilities to otherwise unserviced areas such as Muthetheni and So. Kibaoni.

During this period markets also become more widely dispersed. The official markets had initially been concentrated along major roads and later in areas of higher productivity but by the 1950s most location centers had an area of shops and stalls. New periodic markets had also been established, leading to a much improved coverage of the district (Figure 5.6). Market densities in the highlands usually allowed for easy access (8 km maximum distance) to at least one weekly market and in Iveti location this distance was reduced to one mile. In contrast, market distribution in the lowlands, though improved, was still characterized by gaps in coverage and average distances from homestead to market that made one day round-trips difficult.

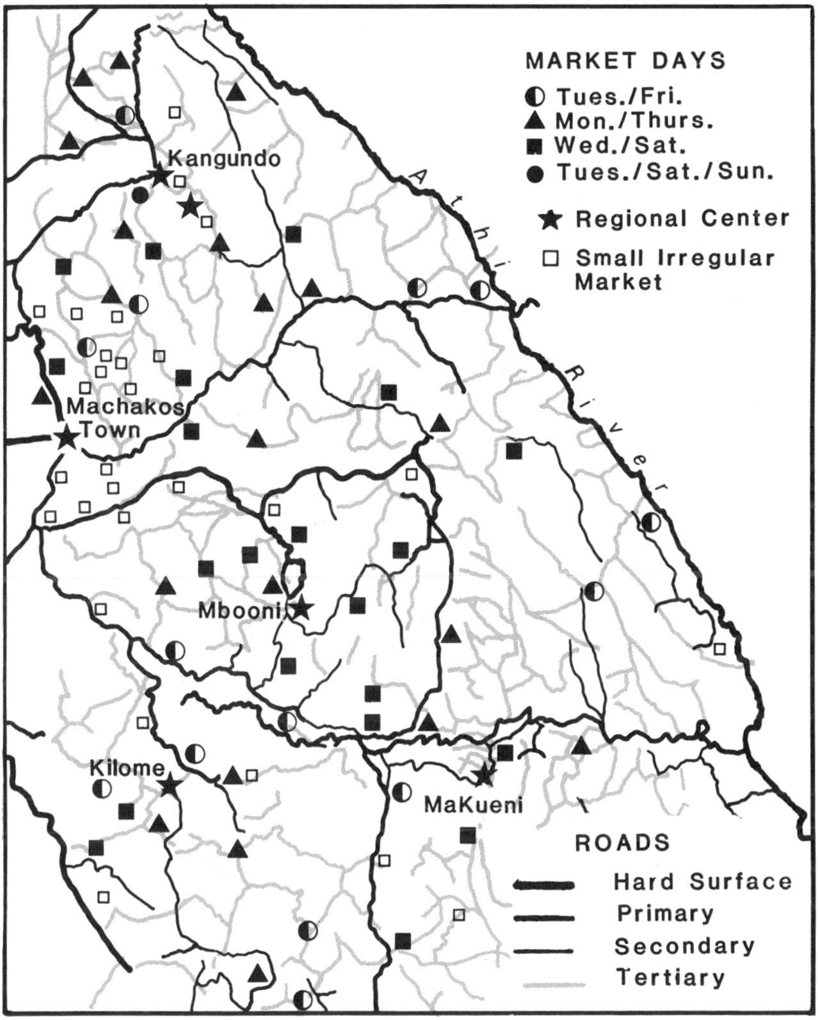

Figure 5.6 Periodic Markets Circa 1955

CHAPTER 5: REFERENCES

[1] Huxley, *A New Earth*, 198.

[2] Kenya Archives, *Annual Agricultural Report*, 1943.

[3] Owako, "Machakos Land and Population," 221.

[4] Huxley, *A New Earth*, 198.

[5] Kenya Archives, *Annual Agricultural Report*, 1949, 12.

[6] Ruthenberg, *Agricultural Policy in Kenya*, 53.

[7] Mitchell, *Agrarian Problems in Kenya*, 24-25.

[8] Ruthenberg, *Agricultural Policy in Kenya*, 56.

[9] Huxley, *A New Earth*, 208.

[10] De Wilde, *Experience with Agricultural Development*, 110.

[11] Ruthenberg, *Agricultural Policy in Kenya*, 6-8.

[12] Kenya Archives, *Annual Agricultural Report*, 1957, 7.

[13] Ibid., 1951, 2.

[14] Owako, "Machakos Land and Population," 257.

[15] Datoo, "Peasant Agricultural Production," 72.

[16] Kenya Archives, *Annual Agricultural Report*, 1952, 11.

[17] Leys, *Underdevelopment in Kenya*, 52.

[18] Kenya Archives, *Annual Agricultural Report*, 1951.

[19] Ibid., 1952, 12.

[20] Ibid., 1959, 20.

[21] Owako, "Machakos Land and Population," 272.

[22] Ibid., 269.

[23] Kenya Archives, *Annual Report*, 1952, 11.

[24] Ibid., 1951, 34.

[25] Ibid., 1954, 55.

[26] Ibid., 1953, 42.

[27] Kenya Archives, *Handing Over Notes, Western Division*, 1957.

CHAPTER 6

POST-INDEPENDENCE: THE FIRST TEN YEARS

1. Government Programs and Policies

The transition from colonial to independent Kenya in 1964 was marked by only one dramatic change in agricultural policy: the partial amalgamation of the European and African farming systems through African resettlement in the scheduled areas (White Highlands) and through cooperative ranching.[1] Other developments were the result of the politically charged atmosphere before and just after independence. For example, non-compliance with conservation regulations had been encouraged by African leaders as an expression of anticolonialism; after the establishment of the Kenya state, it proved difficult to transform this type of activity into cooperation.

Kenyan policies were more supportive of agriculture than those of most African states. Efforts remained focused on increasing export earnings from agriculture through research, farmer services, land registration and controlled resettlement. This was an effective strategy, but only as long as land was available for redistribution. Productivity and smallholder income rose in the 1960s as a result of increased pesticide and fertilizer use, the development of higher yielding crop strains (particularly hybrid maize), and the more efficient and widespread marketing of such cash crops as pyrethrum, coffee, tea, fruits and vegetables, and dairy products.[2] In effect, the programs that had started during the Swynnerton era combined with good weather in the 1960s, appeared to be conducive to improved production figures even in Machakos District.[3]

Yet, in spite of the positive signs of economic growth, some problems were becoming more firmly entrenched. The Kenyan government appeared as unsupportive of the arid and semi-arid areas as its colonial predecessor had been. Only limited efforts were made to ameliorate the impact of the famine of 1971-72 or even that of 1975.[5] Furthermore, there was still no attempt being made to provide an alternative source of income for lowland farmers who lacked a cash crop comparable to those that had succeeded in the hills. It probably would have made sense to encourage the commercial cultivation of hybrid maize in suitable lowland areas. Such a development would have required improved infrastructure, markets, and pricing policies, however, and these were not forthcoming.

The government also underplayed the threat of landlessness. Since the mid 1950s, it had been claimed that the spread of land registration and the encouragement of cash crops would not have negative side effects on poor farmers. Any loss of land was to be offset by increased employment opportunities within a more productive agricultural sector. Unfortunately, this prognosis ignored both the tendency for the number of landless to increase more rapidly than the demand for labor and the fact that the typical on-farm jobs that became available were both seasonal and poorly paid.

The government's satisfaction with the status quo removed any immediate impetus to design or implement new rural development policies. One exception to this lack of interest was the organization of the Kericho Conference of 1966 which discussed the need for 1) a more comprehensive integrated approach to rural development, 2) greater decentralization and 3) more equitably distributed programs that would shift attention to the less well endowed sections of the country where the conditions of rural life had not necessarily improved.[5]

It was not until 1969 and the preparation of the 1970-74 five year plan that some of the themes raised in the Kericho conference were finally incorporated into government policy. Since the conference had covered many topics, yet did not put forth few tangible directives, the five-year plan suffered from a dearth of specific remedies. It did, however, create District Development Committees to facilitate the process of decentralization and it introduced the concept of spatial planning for rural development.[6]

The most concrete initiative to emerge from the 1970-74 development plan was the Special Rural Development Program (SRDP). This project was to become country-wide to include all of the ecological zones but initially it incorporated only six pilot schemes. Each pilot provided a case study for the evaluation of an integrated rural development approach that included farmer training, extension, credit, and the incorporation of local environmental and social conditions into the planning process.[7]

Although the SRDP was well supported at first, the concentration of government effort on just six project areas came to be perceived as an inappropriate use of scarce resources. Ultimately, the combination of inadequate government commitment and a demand for rapid results underminded the program.[8] When several scheduled assessments showed, as expected, a lack of dramatic change, the project activities were severely curtailed.

In 1972, an innovative approach to rural development was put forth but it was never implemented since parts of it were too threatening to the local power structure. The following policies were advocated: 1) the increased use of appropriate technology, improved markets, credit and pricing, and input supply; 2) a concentration on poor families and on the settlement of underutilized land; and 3) land redistribution. The last of the three would have brought about a smaller average farm size which would in turn have facilitated the intensification of agriculture.[9]

Only two new programs were specifically geared to the lowlands, one which focused on augmenting dry season water supplies and a second which was geared to the development of drought resistent crop varieties. With regard to the first goal, new dams were constructed but many of these silted up in a few years. New boreholes were drilled as well only to become sites for severe overgrazing. Part of the problem was insufficient involvement of local people in planning and implementation. In effect, dams or boreholes that were turned over to local authorities were not maintained properly either because maintenance procedures were poorly understood or because of high costs.

More success was experienced in the search for rapidly maturing crops, particularly Katumani Maize. This new variety was considered to be a possible long term solution to the recurrent famine phenomenon in the lowlands but in spite of obvious advantages, Katumani Maize was not being widely adopted as of 1971-73. There were several reasons for farmer reluctance. Most important was the association of Katumani with a package of activities, each of which was necessary to insure the crop's success. The package included proper planting and spacing, thorough weeding, and a level of soil fertility that often called for the application of fertilizer; most farmers could neither supply the labor for weeding nor afford to purchase fertilizer.[10] The first strains of Katumani to be developed also produced less grain than regular maize during seasons that had above average rainfall. Thus, the typical household was still left dependent on low yielding local maize.[11]

The final focus of interest during the early 1970's was the strategy for spatial planning. Kenya was one of the first countries in Africa to employ this strategy in response to a pervasive problem of inaccessibility. The following quandary had emerged by the time of independence: should low levels of transport and services be allowed to persist until increases in productivity and income could support improvements in infrastructure and services, or would productivity not improve until the quality of access was higher? With the 1970-74 plan, the Kenyan government opted to move gradually in the direction of intervention because of the grossly uneven pattern of access to goods and services that characterized most rural regions as well as the excessive rate of rural-urban migration to the largest cities.

The first general spatial planning guidelines were followed by the design of detailed plans for each region. Service centers were identified which would receive government support and which would eventually be linked by improved roads. The centers in each district were to be part of a five-level hierarchy that included at least one urban center at the top and four tiers of smaller towns providing lower order goods and services.

This strategy had two basic purposes. First of all, it was meant to provide a mechanism for overcoming rural isolation either by upgrading existing centers or creating new ones. Secondly, by channeling new public and private investment into officially-designated locations, the government could avoid the spontaneous growth of sub-optimal centers, none of which would contain a full range of needed services.[12] Since the early colonial period, such sub-optimal central places had often emerged within a division; one based on a mission station with its own primary school, a second functioning as an administrative center, and a third based on marketing activities (see Chapter 3). This pattern was inefficient in terms of serving the needs of the rural household and it presented problems when the government wanted to expand all weather roads, piped water supplies, or electrical lines.[13] Whichever center was chosen for these investments, it became necessary to replicate the missing services that were located elsewhere.

In addition to identifying sites for government investment, the plan specified which goods and services should be located at each level in the hierarchy. Few of the designated centers had all of the recommended services as of the early 1970's; it was assumed that they would gradually be acquired so that by the year 2000 the entire package would be in place. The central place system would than include the following components and characteristics.[14]

1. Sub-local and local centers.

These centers were to be located within walking distance of any homestead (1.8 km) and serve approximately 4,000 to 5,000 people. Eventually, services in these centers would include a primary school, dispensary, several shops, a water supply, and possibly a periodic market. They would be connected to higher order centers with at least a minor road and would be most significant in reaching the population of sparsely settled areas.

2. Market centers

This level of the hierarchy was meant to be the focus of local trade. Ideally, market centers would contain a health center, a secondary school, a banking and postal facility, telephone service, and a piped water supply. The trade function of the town would be supported by at least a minor road with a regular bus service and by the establishment of reserved plots for produce markets and other commercial activities. These centers would be located at no more than 8 to 12 km from any occupied land, serving approximately 10-15,000 persons with a resident population of less than 2,000.

3. Rural Center

These towns were meant to be nodal points in the district system of transport and exchange. Here, in addition to the services normally available in a market town, there would be an administrative function, some small rural industry, and a large market. Basic infrastructure would include a sewage disposal system, electricity and access along a secondary road. Approximately 40,000 persons would be served by these towns, each of which would have a population of two to ten thousand.

4. Urban Center

Initially these were to be important district towns or cities occupied by more than 10,000 persons and serving 100 to 150,000 with a complete range of services. Later, a population of 5,000 was substituted as the lower cut-off point for urban centers.

In Machakos District, the selection of towns to be included in the official central place system followed a thorough examination of existing infrastructure, services and service areas. Figure 6.1 includes all of the centers that were initially designated and the level of centrality that they were to achieve by the year 2000. It also shows the location of actual and proposed service areas, each of which was to surround a center designated rural or higher. This plan was reevaluated ten years later and as a result the number of designated centers in each category was increased. The second study took account of a more rapid than expected rate of urbanization and was more attuned to central place theory, national policy, and potential economic growth.[15]

The final product of spatial planning was more highland that lowland oriented. The scheduled upgrading of Masii, Kalawa, and Sultan Hamud (outside the old district boundary) to rural centers was meant to create three new service areas in the lowlands and to reduce the average distance to higher level services. Yet, there was to be at least one market or rural center in each highland location and both Machakos town and Kangundo were scheduled to become full urban centers. In effect, the "core area of the district continues to receive priority in development planning because the capital invested there will get quick results."[16]

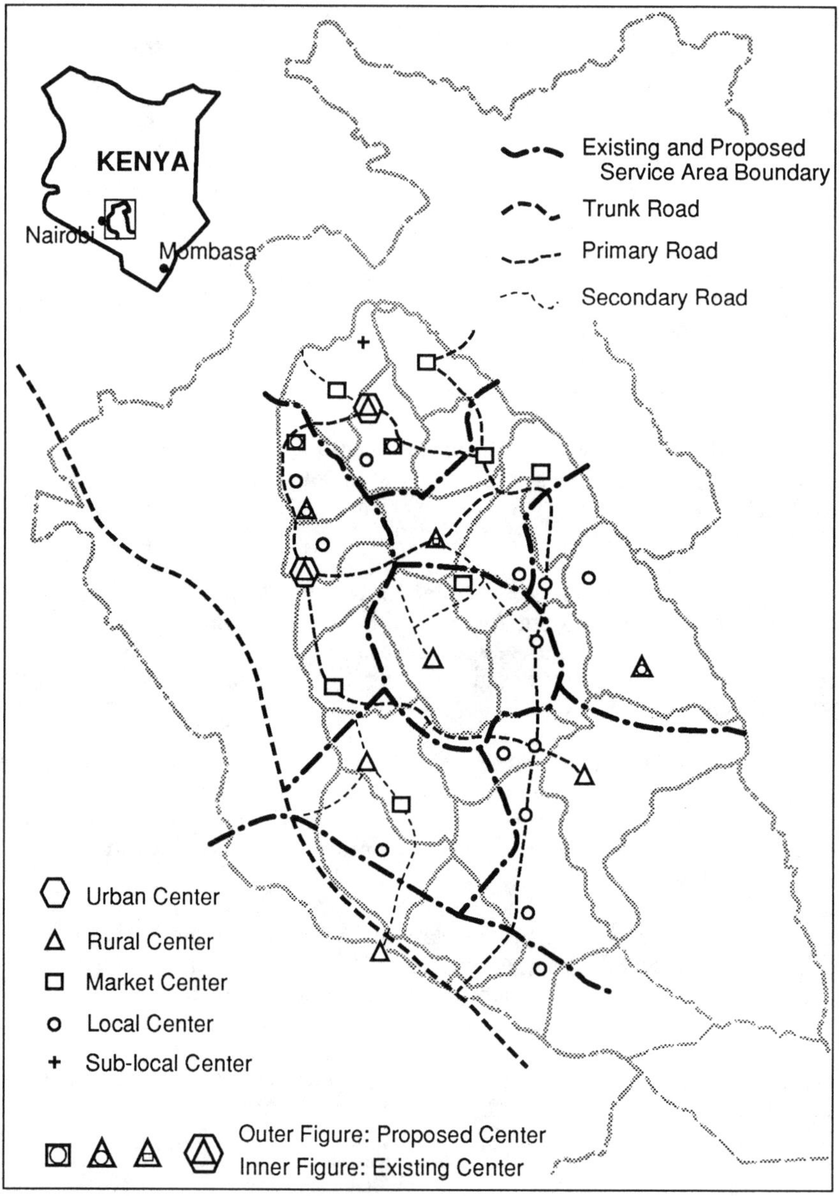

Figure 6.1 Plan for the Year 2000: Service Areas, Service Centers, and Roads

2. Regional Differentiation and the Strategy for Survival

Without effective interjection from the government, the disparity between highland and lowland became more exaggerated. The symbiotic ties which had previously existed between the two areas were disappearing before independence. The lowland had declined into a typical peripheral role, providing the highlands with labor and certain low-priced raw materials (cattle products in particular) and receiving relatively high-priced foodstuffs from the highlands.[17] Other signs of a peripheral relationship were the low wages paid to migrant lowland laborers and the concentration of limited investment funds in highland based projects with their higher immediate returns (see above).[18] Marketing boards and cooperative societies continued to be controlled by and to operate in the interest of large farmers after independence. One result of this type of domination has been that small farmers have been unable to compete for limited supplies of fertilizers and insecticide or were remote from reliable sources of these inputs.

The vulnerable position of the lowlands also intensified as a result of very rapid population growth. In some areas the growth rate had been in excess of thirty-three percent a year, ten times the national average.[19] Many migrants into the area were exiles from the land-scarce highlands who lacked skills appropriate to dryland farming and cattle keeping. Others cultivated land that was unproductive during dry years and would have been better kept in pasture. Choices of crops and techniques were constrained because the need to guarantee subsistence in dry years was more important than maximizing potential income.

The role of indigenous modes of dealing with the problems of survival had dissipated further by the mid 1970s. The relationship of highland and lowland farmers had become primarily one of exploitation rather than of mutually advantageous trade accompanied by sharing during periods of stress. The process of land registration, the subsequent competition for land, and the spread of commercial activities had caused extended family functions to decline so that one could no longer rely on assistance from kin during famines.[20] In their vulnerable position, lowland farmers could anticipate higher prices when food was scarce and especially low wages when there were large numbers of job seekers.

Alternative activities continued to be important to the lowlands during periods of stress, but with substantial limitations; since some of these activities required capital or specialized skills (running a shop, tailoring, carpentry) they were not widely available as survival strategies. Other options were closed off because they were based on access to scarce or expensive raw materials, as in the case of grain for beer-making or firewood for direct sale and charcoal production. Because of these constraints and as a result of the widespread availability of manufactured goods, numerous crafts and established skills were gradually disappearing from the population.

The importance of Kamba rituals for dealing with drought also continued to decline although the more isolated parts of the district experienced the least change. The most important factor in this process was the spread of Christianity. Most locations that had data available were, by 1973, twenty-five percent Christian, although non-involvement in the Kamba religion was even higher than this figure would indicate. A survey carried out in two locations (Mbiuni and Masii) on the use of *Ithembo* for the purposes of preventing illness revealed that only 10% of the population participated in this activity.[21]

The decline of traditional rituals was exacerbated by population growth and the commercialization of sacred land. For example, one *Ithembo* near Machakos town functioned continuously until 1961, but when a flood in the area caused considerable damage, the site was never reestablished. Two other *Ithembo* trees were deserted when some of their branches had to be cut down, in one case because a road was widened, in another because cultivation was expanding and it was deemed essential to expose more of the ground to sunlight.

A final threat to the persistence of *Ithembo* was the aging of the guards and other functionaries who had traditionally been given the responsibility of maintaining the physical site or organizing the rituals. In the author's survey of eight areas, only one active guard had a son who expected to follow his father's occupation. Others talked about lack of interest, the unwillingness to part with goats for sacrifices, and even a tendency, which they deplored, for thieves to steal the sacrificed animals. Certain other aspects of Kamba religious beliefs have endured more easily than the practice of sacrifice, such as the use of fetishes in disease control. The Aimu still appeared but in many Kamba stories they were no longer referred to by name.

The mobility strategy continued to play an important role among the Kamba but under very difficult circumstances. The spreading out of fields was undermined by land consolidation and registration. As for the process of migration, it was also complicated by land scarcities, and a growing tendency for farmers to invest in fixed capital that could not readily be replicated. Under these circumstances, a move by a family to a new location would entail the selection of a potentially marginal or illegal location and a loss of resources.

It is important to note that by the 1960s, increasing mobility had come to reflect the problem of crowding even more than that of drought, although the two motivations for relocation frequently overlapped. The highlands were not only becoming areas of population pressure with increasing land costs and fragmentation, but were also experiencing land deterioration, particularly erosion. Thus, land was becoming less productive at the same time it was more in demand. One response was to move downslope where the average size of holdings was rapidly becoming too small given the limited and erratic precipitation.

An important ramification of rising land values was an increase in the establishment of freehold tenure leading in turn to serious land disputes among relatives, and, ultimately, actual landlessness. Some individuals became the victims of the manipulations of family members: younger brothers who were allocated only marginal plots, sons who were virtually disinherited when their fathers sold off all the family holdings, or divorced women who were left without any legitimate claims to property. Other landless individuals were migrants who for many years had either squatted on European land or lived in cities. When they returned home they found their land rights abrogated, often because a relative had not defended their claims. The problem of landlessness was particularly serious in a society that viewed land ownership as a basic source of status as well as continuity with the past (ancestral spirits, sacred places) and a network of kin and neighbors.

Contention over land rights were complicated by the government role in promoting land registration and consolidation, a process that was accepted relatively slowly in Machakos District. The registration procedures favored the creation of larger holdings and often led to the elimination of marginal plots under two hectares in size. Yet, even without the government role or devious dealings on the part of certain individuals, the process of land subdivision among family members would have resulted in the emergence of substandard plots. These holdings were too small and/or too infertile to function as the basis of even a subsistence system. When faced with the prospect of survival on holdings of just a few acres, rural families had no options other than the permanent or temporary migration of one or more individuals.

Farmers had sometimes anticipated the crisis of inadequate acreage by establishing a satellite farm while their original homesteads were still operable. The use of settlement schemes for this purpose has already been discussed, some of these schemes being located several hundred miles from the main farm. Migrants into Machakos town also tended to retain home shambas. More than half the Machakos workers who owned land within ten miles of the town continued to farm their homestead plot, commuting to town daily by foot, bicycle, or bus. Workers living at greater distance from their farms, often put their holdings in the care of the other family members between home visits.[22]

The number of destinations opened to the would-be migrant without capital to purchase land were rapidly shrinking during the 1960s and early 1970s. One mode of coping with this reality was a new type of squatting--occupying territory to which one had no legal right. Several sites were utilized in this way, including the Chulyu Hills which combined the advantages of fertile soil with the problems of limited surface water and government ownership. According to one interesting study, the typical squatter, eschewing the use of fertilizer or other inputs so as to maximize immediate returns, was faced with rapidly diminishing yields as the resource base deteriorated.[23] Squatters were one of the target groups for priority resettlement, and by 1965 it was estimated that one-third of the registered squatters had been resettled. The strategy provided only temporary relief, however, as new squatters emerged more quickly than they could be placed.

None of the legal options available to the potential migrant have been without shortcomings. In the early 1960s, improved rainfall conditions in southern Machakos resulted in increased interest in Kikumbulyu. Large areas of bush needed to be cleared to make these efforts viable, and numerous colonists were defeated by the labor requirements, persistent tsetse, or the wild animals that could ruin a field of crops. Furthermore, drier interludes followed the wet years, imposing additional burdens on already hard-pressed and often isolated farmers. Yet, even in marginal areas like Kikumbulyu, an end to the ready supply of land could be foreseen. As early as 1965 it was estimated that if 20 acres per family were used as the minimum requirement only 21,837 more farmers could be settled in lower Makueni, Yatta, and Kikumbulyu (Figure 7.1).[24]

3. The Rural Economy: Survey Results from 1974 to 1980

The problems which had emerged in Machakos District by the early 1970s can be better understood by examining selected areas and sample populations in more detail. With this end in mind, the results of three surveys have been compiled and compared. The surveys were carried out over an eight year period somewhat enlarging the time frame, but basically they represent prevailing conditions in the district before or at the time of major current rural development initiatives. The surveys provide an in-depth perspective on rural households, identifying basic cropping and livestock patterns, key constraints of land and labor, and problems of a deteriorating resource base. They also allow for some highland-lowland comparisons in terms of security, crop diversity and relative access to good and services. One of the surveys provides data from Zones III, IV, and V, while the other two focus on the semi-arid areas.

The first of these surveys was prepared and implemented by the author in 1974. It is based on 475 households in six locations (Figure 6.2). Two of the locations, Iveti and Kilungu, are predominantly highland (h), the second two, Kalama and Mitaboni, are mixed highland and lowland, and the third pair, Kimutwa and Muthetheni are almost all lowland (1). The locations also vary according to accessibility: both in terms of distance to Machakos Town and position on the regional road network. Iveti (h) and Kimutwa (l) are both highly accessible while Kilungu (h) and Muthetheni (l) are relatively remote. Kilungu can be reached by one of the major roads of the district but it is the most isolated of the highland areas. Kalama and Mitaboni are intermediate with regard to access.

The second survey was carried out in 1977 as part of a research effort financed by the Agency for International Development to provide background information for the Kenya Arid and Semi-Arid Lands Development Project.[25] The research output was organized into ten separate studies, several of which were of interest, but the source of the critical survey is study No. 6 by Derrick Thom.[26] The survey was based on a sample of 2,332 households in semi-arid locations in both Kitui and Machakos District (Figure 6.2).

The third survey was designed as part of an evaluation of an Integrated Rural Development Project in Machakos District.[27] It was undertaken in 1980 among 326 households in four sublocations. Again, all of the sample came from semi-arid (Zone IV) areas with intermediate accessibility in Kalama, Mbooni, Kiteta, and Ukia locations. The sample consisted of two groups: households who had received credit from the rural development program and those in the same sub-locations who had not received credit.

Each of these studies utilized different sampling methods. In the 1974 survey, the sample was derived from the random selection of homesteads within grid squares laid over four representative areas in each location. Enumerators attempted to locate homesteads close to the designated point on the map with the stipulation that at least fifty households were to be selected from each location. The Meyer's study divided sublocations into neighborhoods within which all resident households were identified by assistant chiefs and elders. Random samples were then drawn from these neighborhoods; 160 households from the credit recipients and 66 from the non-recipients.

The A.I.D. survey assigned enumerators to their home areas. Locations were chosen that were semi-arid to arid with some recent in-migration and with a range of population densities from high to sparsely settled. Actual subjects were chosen randomly using a transect line along an ecological gradient. Three to five sub-locations in each location were to be covered.[28]

All three of these surveys began with a pre-testing of the questionnaire. Questions were translated into the Kamba language and the actual interviewing was carried out by Kamba speakers, who ranged from Form IV

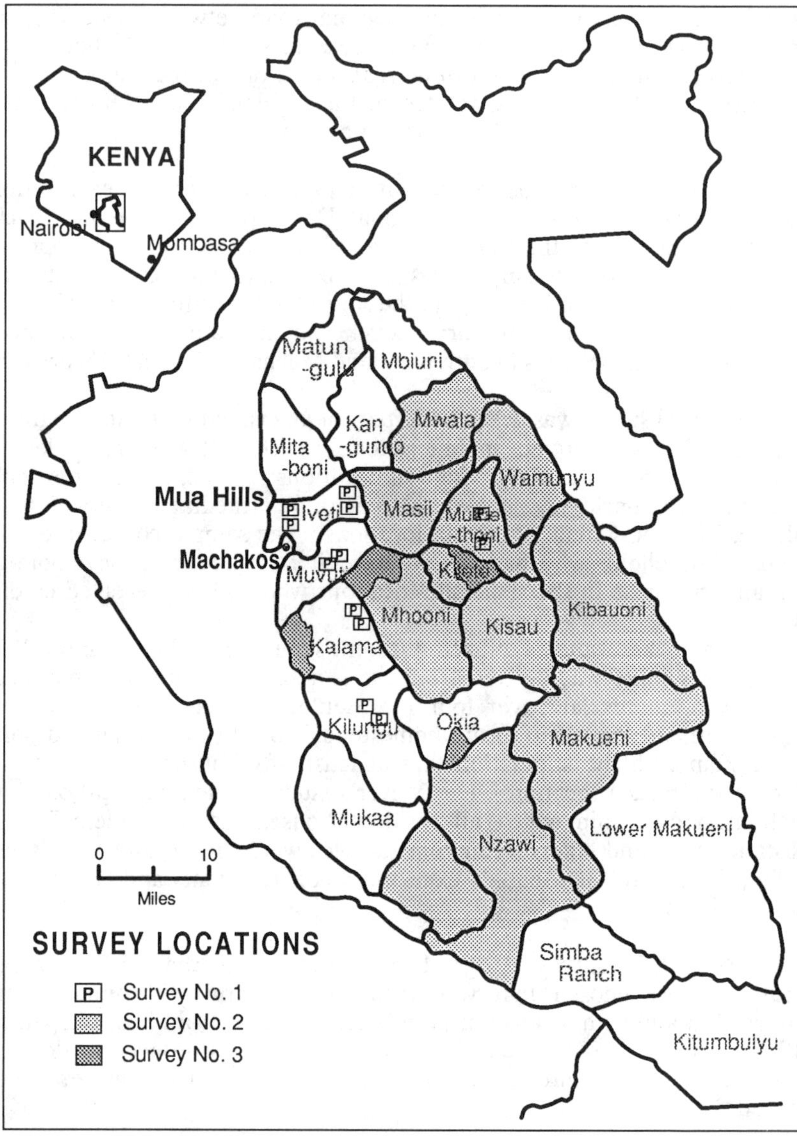

Figure 6.2 Survey Locations

graduates to college students trained in survey research. Whenever possible, field interviewers were accompanied by the primary researcher and/or by an assistant who could measure fields or in other ways confirm or reject the estimates made by household members.

a. The Rural Economy: Land

One of the first themes to be covered in each of these surveys is land ownership in terms of both average size and spatial distribution of holdings. All studies conducted during the last decade (1970-80) refer to land fragmentation and to the shrinking of farm acreage, sometimes below the level required for subsistence productions. According to the AID report which is biased toward lowland conditions, farm size averaged 5.2 ha. (12.95 acres) although 43% of the sample population operated on less than 2.8 ha (7 acres).[29] This figure approximates the results of Meyer's study: 41% of the population owned less than two ha. of land while 69% owned less than 4 ha.[30] The 1974 survey shows a similar pattern but with an average farm size of 3.8 ha. Furthermore, almost 55% of the sampled population owned more than one plot (43.5% and 37% for the AID and Myer's Studies respectively). The mean number of plots in the 1974 survey was 2.9 but there was a variation from highlands to lowlands: the figure for Kilungu (h) was 3.1 while for Muthetheni (l) it was 1.8. This pattern reflects two facets of the highland situation: 1) a greater opportunity to exploit more than one ecological niche and 2) land scarcity leading to frequent sub-division. These multiple plots were usually quite small; in one case two thirds of land fragments were less than 2 ha. (5 acres).[31]

The government program in land registration and consolidation has provided a countervailing force to land fragmentation, but Machakos farmers have historically been more resistant to land registration than farmers in other areas of central Kenya. At the time of the A.I.D study, 43.3% of sample farmers had been registered compared to 80 to 90% in some of the comparable districts. Yet, the process of consolidation may be inexorable since the authorities continue to regard scattered plots as inefficient. They have, in effect, ignored the advantage of multiple plots as part of a strategy to spread out risk.

b. The Rural Economy: Crop and Production

In any given year only part of the total acreage of a homestead was cultivated. On a typical holding of 3.3 ha. (8.3 acres), approximately 51% was used for food crops, 3.6% for cash crops, and the rest was divided into fallow, pasture, and unused land.[32] The food production part of this system was based on four major crops of which maize had been the most important. According to the 1974 survey, maize was grown by between 88 and 100% of the sample during the short rains and by between 66 and 95% during the long rains (Table 6.1). In terms of acreage, the patterns across Machakos District were consistent, at least during the short rains when maize was grown on 40 to 46% of all cultivated land. During the long rains the acreage in maize per farm ranged from 32 to 52% (Table 6.3). According to the agronomic study of the A.I.D. project, maize acreage was stable in some areas and declining slightly in others.[33] It is a crop for which an elaborate marketing mechanism has been developed, but an average of 74% of total production was home consumed.

The second most important food crop in the district was beans and across Machakos District the percentage of the total population growing this crop was comparable to that cultivating maize (Table 6.1). The third and fourth crops were pigeon peas and cowpeas respectively. The agronomic study (A.I.D.) found that the amount of total production of these crops that were home consumed varied from a high of 87% to a low of 54% for the more marketable pigeon peas. All of these pulses seemed to be increasing in importance which augured well for improved diets and soil fertility. Sorghums and millets, on the other hand, have almost disappeared from the cropping scheme in most of Machakos District in spite of their resistance to drought. In the 1974 survey sorghum was not recorded and millet was produced by only an average of 7% of farmers on less than 3% of the cultivated land. The government has experienced little success to date in reviving these crops in part because school children are not available to scare away birds and prevent crop damage. At the present time the relative importance of millet does not correlate with rainfall probabilities since millet had ceased to be grown as a famine-relief crop in semi-arid areas and was as likely to be grown for beer production as for food.

The four major crops accounted for a very substantial part of the total production of the typical Machakos District farm. In the highlands, the percentage of total cultivated land devoted to these crops was lower than the average but it was still 69% in Iveti and 81% in Kilungu. In the lowland division of Muthetheni the percentage increased sharply to 98.85, while the other divisions lay between these extremes. Intercropping was not unusual; as much as 55% of the total maize acreage was intercropped with pigeon peas or cow peas. Another difference between highland and lowland had to do with the relative importance of pigeon and cow peas. Cowpeas were grown by less than 10% of all sampled farmers in Kilungu and Iveti but 25 to 74% of growers in Muthetheni produced cow peas, depending upon the season. Pigeon peas also tended to be more common in the lowlands. Both of these crops, though labor intensive, could usually survive erratic or below average annual precipitation and were thus hedges against drought-related famine.

As a result of a lower average acreage devoted to the basic crops, the highlands have had a greater scope for crop diversity. In Iveti, eight crops

TABLE 6.1

Machakos District Crop Cultivation:
Percentage of Farmers Growing Each Crop

		Short Rains	Long Rains
Growing -	Potatoes	- 19.5 (2)*	27 (2)
	Maize	- 94.9	77.4
	Beans	- 95.7	74.4
	Pigeon Peas	- 33.46	52.7
	Other Peas	- 14 (4)	19.8 (5)
	Millet	- 7.10	4.9 (4)
	Bananas	- 4.5	Same
	Coffee	- 8.15	Same
	Vegetables	- 26.83 (3)	23.2 (3)
	Fruit	- 10.3 (2)	3.3 (2)
	Tomatoes	- 14.4 (4)	5 (3)
	Cabbage	- 18 (3)	6 (4)
	Sweet Potatoes	- 9 (2)	8 (2)
	Tobacco	- 7.25 (4)	26 (3)
	Wheat	- 6 (1)	44 (2)
	Pumpkins	- 9.8 (3)	13 (3)
	Onions	- 6.3 (2)	7.9 (2)
	Papaya		11.5 (7)
	Cassava	- 3 (1)	7.5 (2)
	Rice		6 (1)
	Cotton	- 2.2 (1)	28 (1)
	Mangoes		6 (1)
	Sugar Cane	- 15.2 (3)	14.75 (4)

Source: 1974 Survey of six locations
*(2) Indicates that the crop is only grown in two locations (percentage of growers in these locations only)

TABLE 6.2

Percentage of Total Acreage Planted in Four Basic Crops

	Maize	Beans	Pigeon Peas	Peas	Total
Kilungu					
short rains	41.8	35.9	2.2	.8	80.7
long rains	46.0	32.2	2.8	.6	81.6
Iveti					
short rains	46.0	20.0	3.8	1.0	70.8
long rains	48.0	16.0	3.8	67.8	
Kalama					
short rains	44.0	30.0	16.0	1.3	91.3
long rains	37.0	31.2	16.0	1.7	85.9
Mitaboni					
short rains	44.6	31.1	15.0	.9	92.8
long rains	32.0	23.0	15.0		90.0
Kimutwa					
short rains	44.7	32.0	10.0	2.3	89.0
long rains	32.0	15.0	10.0	7.6	64.6
Muthetheni					
short rains	44.7	33.1	15.0	6.1	98.9
long rains	37.3	27.0	18.7	15.8	98.8

were cultivated in addition to the basic grains, beans, and peas to include bananas, coffee, vegetables, and fruits of various types (Tables 6.3 and 6.4). Similarly, Kilungu farmers grew seven additional crops. Kimutwa and Mitaboni farmers, in part because of proximity to markets, grew nine and eleven crops respectively. In Kalama the number was reduced to one during the short rains and five during the long rains, while Muthetheni farmers grew only three crops other than the basics and these in very small amounts.

It is possible to compare the relative importance of each crop at three time intervals for Machakos as a whole (1970, 1974, and 1978 projected), with the 1974 survey figures for two locations, Iveti and Kalama (Table 6.5). Maize acreage, as expected from earlier discussions, decreased as a percentage of total acreage between 1970 and 1974 and then remained somewhat stable. The Machakos-wide figures were in all cases higher than the results for either Iveti or Kalama alone. Beans, cowpeas, and pigeon peas showed an increase from 1970 to 1974 and correlated more closely with the Kalama than the Iveti figures. Sorghums and millets showed little change as did cash crops with the exception of coffee which increased in importance. These figures indicate quite clearly that, in Machakos as a whole, cash crops were an almost insignificant component of crop acreage. They were usually placed on small plots and cultivated last. Only when individual locations were examined did a particular crop of local importance stand out as in Iveti (coffee) and Kalama (cotton). Sunflower seed was negligible in the 1974 study, but it has since expanded in drier areas, sometimes at the expense of cotton.

In all of Machakos District animals formed an important component of the subsistence system and as much as one third of subsistence requirements could be derived from livestock. According to the 1974 survey, 67.3% of the sample population kept chickens for meat and eggs on a regular basis. This concurs with the AID findings which point to chickens being fairly ubiquitous (they are owned by at least 50% of the population in any location). Goats were also widespread. The 1974 survey shows 63% of the sampled farmers in Kilungu owning goats as opposed to 78% in Muthetheni, indicative of an orientation toward the drier areas. The Myer's study points to a slightly lower average district figure of 59%. The average number of goats per family ranged form 3.2 to 6.3 in 1974 in the locations mentioned above compared to 5.4 average found by Myers. Sheep were also owned in many of these locations but not as often as goats.

In all locations except for Iveti more people were likely to own cattle than goats, with the highest percentage and the largest number of cattle per family in the lowlands. In Muthetheni, 95% of the sample owned cattle as compared to Myer's overall figure of 87%. The average number of cattle per household varied from highlands to lowlands (2.9 and 2.6 in Kilungu and Iveti respectively to 4.6 and 7.3 in Kalama and Muthetheni) reflecting

TABLE 6.3

Comparison of Crops Cultivated Across Locations: Short Rains

	Percentage of Population Cultivating Each Crop					
Crops	Kilungu	Iveti	Kalama	Mitaboni	Kimutwa	Muthetheni
Potatoes	15.0	10				
Maize	88.8	100	97	90.2	95	100
Beans	93.8	100	96	90.2	94.6	100
Pigeon Peas	19.3 (3)	32	17 (3)	75.7	28.8	43
Cow Peas	9.2	4	6.5 (2)	3.5	20 (2)	25
Millet	4 (1)	16	9 (2)	8.7	9.8	
Bananas	6 (1)	16			12 (1)	
Coffee	6.3 (3)	24				
Vegetables	18	8		7.5 (3)		
Fruits	10.6 (3)					1
Tomatoes	18 (3)			8.5 (2)	18 (3)	
Cabbage	36 (3)			15 (1)		
Sweet Potatoes		8			8 (3)	
Tobacco	9 (1)	8		.8 (1)	.5	
Wheat	6 (1)					
Pumpkin				12.3 (3)	14 (1)	
Onions	9.7					
Sugar Cane	18	12		5.5 (2)		
Papaya						
Cassava				3		
Rice						
Cotton						
Mango						

TABLE 6.4

A Comparison of Crops Cultivated Across Locations: Long Rains

Crops	Kilungu	Iveti	Kalama	Mitaboni	Kimutwa	Muthetheni
	Percentage of Population Cultivating Each Crop					
Potatoes	35	10				
Maize	95	80	76	85	66.8	95
Beans	93	72	73	85	32	100
Pigeon Peas	11 (3)	60	50	8 (1)	63	100
Cow Peas	6 (1)	4	27 (2)		17	74
Millet	7 (3)	28	5.9		3.3	3
Bananas	6	40			12 (1)	
Coffee	6	12				
Vegetables	12 (3)			8 (2)		
Fruits	9 (3)	4				1
Tomatoes		12	3 (1)	4 (1)	10.5	
Cabbage	7.5 (2)	8	4 (1)	10 (2)		
Sweet Potatoes		8			10 (3)	
Tobacco	25 (1)			41.25	6 (1)	
Wheat	58 (1)				31	
Pumpkin			7 (1)	8 (1)	24 (1)	
Onions	7.8	12		8		
Sugar Cane	22 (2)		1 (1)			
Papaya	8 (1)	16		15 (1)		
Cassava	12 (1)	4	3 (3)		8.5 (2)	
Rice	6 (1)					
Cotton			28			
Mango			6			

TABLE 6.5

Crop Productions: Percentage of Total Acreage in Each Crop

Agronomic Survey*-Machakos District Project**				1974 Survey	
	1970	1974	1977	Iveti	Kalama
Sisal	?	1.76	1.5		
Sugar Cane	?	.5	.4	2.8	.2
Cotton	3.7	.5	.4		10.3
Sunflower	-	-	neg.		
Coffee	1.0	1.18	2.3	13.3	
Castor	.18	.18	neg.		
Cereals					
Maize					
Katumani	13.1	22.3	47.5		
L. White	49.3	29.8	5.1		
Both	62.4	52.1	52.6	47	40
Sorghum	.5	.3	.4		
Millet	.5	.18	.6	2.2	1.1
Veg.					
Beans	21.1	23	23	18	30
Cowpeas	3.5	6.6	4.9	1.0	1.5
Pig. Peas	4.5	11.6	11.5	3.8	16
Grams	1.8	1.8	1.3		
Cassava	.4	.27	.6	.3	.2
Potatoes				.9	
Bananas				1.2	
Vegetables				4.5	
Fruit				.4	
Tomatoes				1.4	
Cabbage				1.4	
Tobacco				3.0	
Pumpkin					1.4

* Excludes fruits, vegetables, bananas, wattle.

** Source: MANN, Report No. 2, Table 2.1.

differences in the role of cattle as insurance against crop failure. Keeping cattle in the highland was complicated by farm consolidation and a decline in pasturage that has accompanied population growth.

Cattle were also important as a source of milk although Kamba cows were not good producers in terms of total quantity of milk or the length of the lactation period. Cattle were sources of manure as well, but even though a large number of farmers used some manure for soil fertilization, application might be limited to a small garden plot. In general, livestock had not been well integrated with crop production systems and only about half of all farmers used crop residues for livestock feed.

As the pattern of crop selection indicates, the typical Machakos rural household in 1975 was still subsistence oriented and likely to consume at least three fourths of its own production. Most labor was family based and seeds were usually obtained locally to include a residue from the previous year's harvest. This situation persisted because it was so difficult to increase productivity, diversify, or produce for the market. Any of these adaptations either carried too high a level of risk, made too many demands on limited resources, or required greater access to services and markets.

Shortage of capital was one of the most important constraints. A typical farmer had little income to purchase needed inputs or equipment or to hire laborers. A viable credit system would have eased this situation but credit was most readily available to farmers who had already had a proven record as commercial growers, those who had some formal education, or those who were accessible to the centrally based marketing system. Thus, the subsistence farmer could not break out of the cycle of low income leading to low levels of production, limited surplus, and marginal cash returns.

One approach that has traditionally been used to raise incomes has been the expansion of the numbers of acres cultivated. This strategy becomes difficult when income is inadequate (as mentioned above), when land becomes a commodity in a monetized economy, and/or when population growth leads to the occupation of all the cultivable land in a given region. A second constraint on increasing average farm size was the combination of insufficient family labor and a hoe-based or limited plow-based technology. The typical farm family was characterized by a high dependency ratio whereby women, children, and the elderly remained on the farm while men between the ages of twenty and forty-five migrated to areas of potential employment. Income from such employment could sometimes be used to hire laborers (to be discussed further in the next chapter) but generally, as little as one half hectare per adult might be cultivated in a single year under these circumstances.[34]

The full impact of labor and capital shortage on crop production can be best examined in the context of the annual farm calendar. The distribution of production-related tasks throughout the year is shown in Table 6.6 for a semi-arid area in which basic food crops were supplemented by cotton and sunflower. Because of the double rainy season, crops were cultivated and harvested twice leaving few gaps in the work schedule. Two of the crops, pigeon peas and cotton, were cultivated throughout the year and often overlapped in their demands with other crops that matured more rapidly.

The first major activity of the agricultural year was land preparation and planting. It has been demonstrated that late planting can substantially decrease yields because rainfall tends to be concentrated in period of no more than eight weeks while the evapo-transpiration demand of the growing plant increase well beyond that period. A plant experiencing stress at critical stages of its growth would probably be stunted. Yet, in spite of this phenomenon, planting was frequently delayed because of a shortage of labor.

A second demanding task that impacts strongly on yields is weeding. Since weeds compete with crops for soil nutrients and moisture, insufficient weeding causes substantial production losses. For example, a two week delay in weeding can depress yields by one-third.[35] Finally, the harvesting period represents a third stage during which a labor bottleneck can be experienced. When several crops mature simultaneously, an incomplete harvest usually results.

Given the labor shortfalls that occur during the cultivation cycle, one of the more direct approaches to improving productivity would be to expand plow-based agriculture. As of 1978, agronomist on the AID team estimated that only 10% of the land but 30% of the farms were still based completely on hoe preparation.[36] Approximately 60% of families owned oxen but only 42% actually used animal tillage.[37] The discrepancy was the result of the shortage of trained plow oxen. During the period of peak demand, farmers who habitually rented or exchanged oxen might be forced to wait past the ideal planting time.[38] Oxen were also less efficient after frequent use or when the ground was hard and dry just before the rains. The 1974 survey indicated that 30 to 50% of the sample population in the highlands used oxen at least some of the time while in the lowlands, with more land to prepare and more opportunity to provide grazing, usage ranged from 25 to 90%.

In summary, the image which emerges of the Machakos farm unit in the early to mid 1970s is one of small plots decreasing in size, excessive reliance on maize, limited crop diversity, especially in the lowlands, severe constraints on commercialization of agriculture, and sub-optimum production systems which resulted in depressed yields.

TABLE 6.6

The Annual Farm Calendar

Month		Activities
October	Short Rains	Land Preparation--maize, beans, pigeon peas, cow peas, millet, sorghum, sunflower, cotton Planting--maize, beans, pigeon peas, cow peas, millet, sorghum, sunflower, cotton
November		Weeding
December		Weeding
January	Hot, Dry	Harvest--maize, beans, cow peas, sunflower Weeding--cotton Pesticide Application--cotton
February		Harvest--millet, sorghum Marketing--maize, beans, cow peas, sunflower
March	Long Rains	Land Preparation--maize, beans, millet, sorghum, sunflower Planting--maize, beans, millet, sorghum, sunflower Weeding--pigeon peas
April		Weeding
May		Weeding
June		Weeding
July	Dry	Harvest--pigeon pease, maize, beans, millet, sorghum, sunflower, cotton Marketing--surplus crops Community Activities--constructing schools, terraces, access roads, wells
August		Harvest--cotton Marketing--surplus crops, cotton, sunflower Community Activities
September		Community Activities--Bush clearing by organized groups Land Preparation

Source: Thom, 1978:63, Table 15.

c. The Rural Economy: Population and Resources

The surveys were also able to provide a quantitative dimension to the local perception of constraints on agricultural production. Food shortages continued to plague Machakos District into the late 1970s. One estimate for the number of days for which adequate food was not available in at least one area of the district was 180 or approximately one-half the year.[39]

Almost all Machakos farmers agreed that they had been adversely affected by weather conditions, especially water shortfalls. In the 1974 survey, the most frequently mentioned problems in the agricultural sphere were drought (38%), insect pests and crops diseases (30%), and erosion (20%). Land shortages and poor soil were mentioned by an average of 15% of the respondents, the former being critical in the highlands the latter in the lowlands. In the Meyer's survey, people were asked what prevented income augmentation and the three most frequent answers were inadequate labor (23%), insufficient rain (16%), and insufficient land.[40]

In dealing with these problems farmers indicated that established mechanisms for survival were still important but less effective, as previously indicated. According to the 1974 survey, mutual assistance among friends and relatives had once been a significant component of the survival system (30 percent of respondents claiming that it was a very important source of food during famines) but it had declined in importance.

Alternative employment was still seen as a mode of dealing with poor harvests although most farmers interviewed in the AID study did not perceive that there were any viable long-term alternatives to agriculture. Similarly, most Machakos District farm families (93%) felt that outmigration was no longer a solution to the problems of food shortages, an assessment based on both the hazards of migration as well as the dearth of resettlement sites. The consensus seemed to be that short-term options were still available to include seasonal farm labor or stints of off-farm employment.

With the decline of many traditional adjustments to drought and related problems, farmers were tending to rely more on control of the water supply. It had become more common for farmers to diversify their water sources, especially during the dry season utilizing springs, dams, and, most frequently, water beneath the sand of dry river bottoms (Plate 3). Deep wells, boreholes and limited water storage were also important to selected farmers. Table 6.7 indicates the responses to questions about preparation for future droughts.[41] The response "nothing" may be somewhat misleading since it probably implies nothing in addition to the to the normal rainfall related activities that are part of the typical agricultural year. Other than this response, reactions are a bit diffuse. This data refers mainly to the lowlands where, according to the 1974 survey, responses to water shortfalls

TABLE 6.7

Farmers' Preparation for Future Droughts:
Alternative Strategies

Response to question: "How are you preparing for future droughts?"	Number of Persons	Percent
Nothing	875	38.2
Buying more land	204	8.9
Keeping more animals	116	5.0
Working away from the farm	232	9.9
Preparing soil	103	4.4
Cultivating more land	95	4.1
Storing food	123	5.3
Improving farm	93	4.0
Other	452	20.2
	2,293	100.0

Source: Thom, 1978:79, Table 24.

PLATE 3. A Water Source Excavated in a Dry River Bed

remained more diverse and important than in the highlands.

One of the problems with obtaining water had always been distance to dry season supplies. The diversification of sources had made this less of an issue but, as indicated in Table 6.8, dry season water could still be located at a distance of four kilometers or more for almost half the rural population. Obtaining and carrying water remains one of the more onerous tasks that is usually assigned to women (Plate 4).

While drought had persisted as an ongoing issue, erosion had become more relevant through time. Both the AID and the 1974 survey show that farmers were becoming more aware of erosion although they often believed that terracing alone was sufficient to remove any threat to the soil base. Farmers also saw the connection between erosion and decreasing soil fertility (65% did so) but they were as likely to associate erosion with natural conditions (rainfall, steep slopes, wind, etc.) as with poor farm management. They seemed to be especially reluctant to consider overgrazing as a threat to soil stability.[42] Deforestation was also seen as a major problem but again there was not always a willingness or ability to apply the necessary capital or labor needed to decrease the threat.

d. The Rural Economy: Access to Goods and Services

Improvements in the production system were also hampered by the problem of inaccessibility. When farmers couldn't readily obtain inputs, extension advice, other basic goods and services, or market their surplus output, they could not increase production even in response to improved seeds, prices, or technologies.

At the same time that ambitious plans were being devised to upgrade the service network of the district, the surveys showed the actual level of accessibility in Machakos in the early 1970s to be uneven and often inadequate. There were still too few feeder roads in the transport network and an insufficient number of scheduled buses and trucks. The number of periodic markets had continued to increase gradually (Figure 5.6) but some met only irregularly and there were still wide gaps in the lowlands. It was not unusual in a lowland location for a round trip to market to require headloading produce over a distance of forty kilometers. Under these circumstances, the cash economy was said to function effectively only within a strip three to four kilometers on either side of an all-weather road; beyond this distance the typical smallholder could only market goods on an irregular basis.[43] Two markets are illustrated in Plates 5 and 6, the large bi-weekly market in Machakos town and a smaller market in the Iveti hills that combined a few permanent shops and services with open spaces for produce sellers who gathered at least once each week. Other local services had

TABLE 6.8

Distance to Water

One Way Distance	Dry Season (percent in distance category)	Wet Season (percent in distance category)
Less than 1 km	11.2	28.6
1-3 km	39.9	52.2
4-6 km	23.6	14.0
7-9 km	11.1	2.5
10-12 km	7.3	1.4
13-14 km	1.5	.2
15-20 km	4.4	.1
Over 20 km	1.0	.1
Total	100.0	100.0

Source: Hash and Mbatha, Table 20.

PLATE 4: A Kilungo Woman Carrying Pottery Water Vessels

PLATE 5. Bi-weekly Market, Machakos Town

PLATE 6. Ngelani (Iveti) Market

improved due to both self-help initiatives and government investment. It must be kept in mind, however, that the quality of services varied substantially. Problems of marginal facilities were most likely to occur in remote locations, especially when buildings were constructed by self-help groups without any arrangement for long-term financing. The government was only able to provide personnel and sometimes inputs for approximately 30% of self help (*Harambee*) schools and sometimes less for other types of services.

As of the mid 1970s the highland still retained its favorable position with the regard to access. Table 6.9 shows the distribution of secondary schools and health facilities at the time of the survey of the Eastern Regional Plan in 1970. Most locations had built self help secondary schools, but the highland concentration remained strong. In the realm of health care, a concentration of high level facilities in the highlands was mitigated by more readily available basic health care at dispensaries. These facilities had become much more widespread since the 1950s when only four dispensaries operated in the intermediate areas and only three in the lowlands (Table 5.5.). In 1970 all lowland locations had at least one dispensary (Table 6.9).

By the time of the A.I.D. survey, the situation had improved further for the lowlands. Table 6.10 summarizes the distribution of schools, health facilities, coops, and taxis in terms of the average number of square kilometers covered by each service, activity, or center. The contrast between primary and secondary schools is instructive; the highlands had a primary school for every 3.7 square kilometers, the intermediate areas for every 7 square kilometers, and the lowlands for every 11.8 square kilometers. Although access was better in the highlands, the average maximum distance to school for a lowland student (3.4 km) could be covered on foot by most students. For high schools, however, tributary areas were much larger, increasing from highlands to intermediate areas to lowlands from 20.2 to 49.3 to 156.2 square kilometers respectively. The figures for average population per school showed greater equity across the district and indicate, at least for elementary schools, an improving opportunity of lowland families to avail themselves of basic schooling.

One service factor not included in Table 6.10 is access to agricultural extension personnel. This data is summed up in Table 6.11 which shows an extension service that has reached into all corners of the district, although highland locations tend to have above the average number of officers per location especially in Kangundo and Mbooni. Also included in Table 6.10 is the combined service factor. This measurement pulls together access to a range of goods and services: number of square kilometers and number of persons per butcher, tailor, teashop, bar, fertilizer agent, and fixed pump gas supply. The results show that in intermediate and lowland areas these services were relatively widely dispersed but that there is not much difference in the number of people covered by a service areas. The services included

TABLE 6.9

Health Care Facilities and Secondary Schools by Location: 1970

	Health Care			Secondary Schools	
	Hospitals	Clinics	Dispen-saries	Regular Government	Harambee (Self help)
Highlands					
Iveti	1			2	4
Mitaboni			1		1
Kangundo	1			1	5
Matungulu			1	2	3
Kilungu	1	1	1	2	3
Mbioni		1	1	2	
Intermediate					
Kalama			1		1
Maputi			1	1	
Masii		1			1
Okia			2		1
Mwala			1		
Mbiuni			1	1	1
Kiteta			1		
Lowlands					
Wamunyu			1		
Makueni			1	1	
Nzaui			2		2
Mbitini			2		1
Mukaa			3		2
Muthetheni			1		1
Kisau			1		
Kibauoni			1		

TABLE 6.10

Availability of Selected Services in Highland, Intermediate, and Lowland Locations

	Highlands	Intermediate	Lowlands
sq. kil./coop	87.5	135.6	347.5
pop./coop	51,128.8	19,461.3	31,847.5
sq. kil./primary school	3.7	7	11.8
pop./primary school	1,083.03	1,041.4	902.79
sq. kil./sec. school	20.2	49.3	156.2
pop./sec. school	3,958.6	6,330.3	10,813.8
sq. kil./dispensary	157	148	253
pop./dispensary 42,823	21,378	16,205	
sq. kil./clinic	123	346	1,266
pop./clinic	307	49,882	84,361
sq. kil./hospital	276	1,137	3,766
pop./hospital	74,942	149,646	243,083
sq. kil./taxi	15.4	41.2	97.9
pop./taxi	3,730.9	3,285.8	5,305.4
Combined service			
Factor (C.S.F.)			
sq. kil/C.S.F.	1.6	2.4	5.8
pop./C.S.F.	435	346	389.9

Source: Interpolated from several surveys in the A.I.D. Study, Thom, 1978.

TABLE 6.11

Extension Staff Locations, 1976/77

Division	A.A.0.	A.0.	Location		T.A.	JAA
Kangundo	1	2	(H)	Kangundo	2	9
			(H)	Matungulu	2	7
			(I)	Mwala	2	2
			(I)	Mbiuni	1	3
					7	21
Central	1	1	(H)	Iveti	3	4
			(I)	Muputi	1	5
			(I)	Masii	2	4
			(L)	Wamunyu	2	3
			(H)	Mitaboni	2	4
					10	20
			(H)	Mbooni	3	8
			(L)	Kibauni	1	2
Eastern	1	1	(L)	Kisau	1	2
			(L)	Muthethani	1	3
			(I)	Kiteta	1	3
					7	18
			(L)	Mukaa	1	6
			(H)	Kilungu	3	5
Western	1	1	(I)	Kalama	2	3
			(I)	Okia	2	3
					8	17
			(L)	Makueni	4	9
Makueni	2	1	(L)	Nzaui	2	2
			(L)	Mbitini	1	5
					7	16
TOTALS			21 Locations		39	92
			Average per location		1.8	4.4

AAO Assistant Agricultural Officer
AO Agricultural Officer
TA Technical Assistant
JAA Junior Agricultural Assistant

in this overview are in general more available than schools and health facilities, indicating a market response to potential customers in advance of the placement of government subsidized activities.

CHAPTER 6: REFERENCES

[1] Cone and Lipscomb, *The History of Kenyan Agriculture*.

[2] Kitching, *Class and Economic Change in Africa*, 321.

[3] Lynam, "An Analysis of Risk in Farming," 61.

[4] Heyer et al., *Rural Development in Tropical Africa*, 116.

[5] Sheffield, *Education, Employment and Rural Development*.

[6] Republic of Kenya, *Kenya Development Plan*, 1970-74.

[7] Heyer, Ireri, and Morris, *Rural Development in Kenya*.

[8] Lele, *The Design of Rural Development*, 22.

[9] United Nations, I.L.O., "Employment, Incomes, and Equality," 1745.

[10] Hunt, "Poverty in Semi-Arid Kenya," 84.

[11] DeWilde, *Experience with Agricultural Development*, 89.

[12] Government of Kenya (GOK), Ministry of Land and Settlement, *Human Settlements*, 67.

[13] Taylor, "Spatial Aspects of Rural Development Policy," 182.

[14] GOK, *Eastern Province Regional Development Plan*.

[15] GOK, Ministry of Land and Settlement, *Human Settlements*, 85.

[16] GOK, *Eastern Province Regional Development Plan*, II-2.

[17] Wisner, "Peasants of Tharaka Division," 356.

[18] Porter, *Food and Development in East Africa*, 55.

[19] Mbithi and Wisner, "Drought and Famine in Kenya," 10.

[20] Wisner, "An Overview of Drought in Kenya," 58.

[21] Thomas, "Community Adaptation to Health Services," 3.

[22] Lang, "Urbanization in Machakos," 6.

[23] Mbithi and Barnes, *Spontaneous Settlement in Kenya*, vii.

[24] Owako, "Machakos Land and Population Problems," 280.

[25] U.S. Agency for International Development (USAID), Palmer et al., Pre-Investment Inventory.

[26] Ibid., Thom, "Resources and Social Characteristics."

[27] USAID, Meyer, "Organization of Rural Development."

[28] USAID, Pre-Investment Inventory, Thom, "Resources and Social Characteristics," 71-2.

[29] Ibid., 77.

[30] USAID, Meyer, "Organizational of Rural Development," 90.

[31] USAID, Pre-Investment Inventory, Thom, "Resources and Social Characteristics," 76.

[32] USAID, Pre-Investment Inventory, Mann, "Agronomy," 75.

[33] Ibid., Table 2.9.

[34] USAID, Pre-Investment Inventory, Hash and Mbatha, "Economics," 5.2.

[35] Lynam, "An Analysis of Risk in Farming," 144.

[36] USAID, Pre-Investment Inventory, Hash and Mbatha, "Economics," 5.2.

[37] USAID, Pre-Investment Inventory, Thom, "Resources and Social Characteristics," 77.

[38] Lynam, "An Analysis of Risk in Farming," 143.

[39] USAID, Pre-Investment Inventory, Thom, "Resources and Social Characteristics," 78.

[40] USAID, Meyer, "Organization of Rural Development," 93.

[41] USAID, Pre-Investment Inventory, Thom, "Resources and Social Characteristics," 79.

[42] Ibid., 77.

[43] USAID, Pre-Investment Inventory, Hash and Mbatha, "Economics," 51.

CHAPTER 7

THE FINAL AMALGAMATION

1. New Initiatives in Rural Development

By the mid-1970s it had become obvious that Kenyan development policies had not come to grips with several deepening national issues, particularly those of persistent poverty and inequity. The interrelated crises of the rural areas were deepening as rapid population growth led to shrinking farms, continuous cropping, and migration into marginal areas. All three of these phenomena were in turn promoting erosion, soil nutrient loss, and, ultimately, a decrease in per capita food production. Some of these problems had occurred previously, but never at such a high level of population density.[1]

In order to deal with these challenges and the approximately one million people living in the district, the government begun to pursue two major shifts in national policy. First came a serious questioning of the established approach whereby peasant economic systems and technologies were to be replaced with direct transfers from the industrialized countries. Instead, rural development specialists were finally acknowledging the basic rationality of indigenous household production systems given the prevailing resources base and isolation. The search began in earnest for methods of combining selected components of both peasant farming and modern agriculture.

Simultaneously, a second component of the government strategy was being reexamined: the support for and subsidy of the high potential areas in order to maximize immediate returns while allowing the lowlands to either stagnate or deteriorate. By 1974-6, the semi-arid areas were in no position to function as a frontier province for downslope migration, yet this is the role they had been forced play due to a dearth of alternatives for the inhabitants of the crowded hills. According to one study, the stream of landless migrants being forced to leave high potential areas were becoming concentrated in areas that had no investment to deal with the influx.[2] The government was finally having to concede that "the high potential land is now so heavily populated, it is necessary to consider more and more of the so-called marginal areas."[3]

It was about this time that the International Labor Organization issued a report criticizing, among other things, the long standing disparities between high and low potential areas.[4] The report supported the concept of policy reform including the design of new programs appropriate for the semi-arid areas. In effect, the ILO report, combined with a growing awareness in Kenya of environmental problems, gave rise to the third development plan (1974-1978), the first to pay serious attention to both indigenous production systems and to the less-developed lowlands (henceforth referred to as the ASALS, or the Arid and Semi-Arid Lands).[5] The 1978-1983 plan further reinforced this commitment. It called for long-term planning rather than crisis management to deal with issues like land rehabilitation and the expansion of water resources.

The new government orientation required the mobilization of donor assistance for research on all aspects of farming systems including average size of holdings, the availability of equipment and labor, crop selection, and the physical environment. This information could then be used to identify land and labor constraints and to devise alternative strategies for organizing household labor or affordable technologies to overcome labor bottlenecks. At the same time, long-term equity needs were to be served by providing the medium and low potential areas with a minimum level of services combined with results of agronomic research on drought resistant crops.

In Machakos District, the government program took the form of an integrated rural development program or IRD, based on the assumption that a number of mutually reinforcing investments in a given rural area would make it possible to overcome the prevailing conditions of poverty. Although IRD projects have not been greeted with universal approval, the idea was enjoying considerable positive attention in the mid 197Os and it seemed a logical choice for those areas which needed to be jolted out of a moribund condition.

Integrated programs have actually ranged from loose associations of sectoral projects within one region to extremely complex and tightly coordinated efforts made by specially created administrative units. The Machakos District IRD (known as the Machakos Integrated Development Program or MIDP) represented an intermediate position on this continuum and was the first district-wide IRD program in Kenya. Officially, the district was selected because it contained both marginal agricultural areas and a relatively large population, but it was probably also important that the area was ethnically homogenous and close to Nairobi.[6] Foreign assistance was provided by the European Economic Community (EEC) in the form of a $24 million investment. The initial four year program effectively commenced in 1978-79 although the project was not fully operative until 1980.

The basic goals of the MIDP project were to increase the income of farm households--and augment essential infrastructure and services in selected areas of Machakos District, primarily but not entirely in the lowlands. These interventions were then expected to provide additional employment and investment opportunities, bringing the lowlands into the mainstream of the national economy. To achieve these ends, specific activities were to be undertaken including 1) supporting a more productive agriculture through farmer training, extension, and crop development, research, and the provision of physical and social infrastructure, and 2) improving the resource base by expanding water storage and delivery, soil conservation, grazing management and afforestation. Small industry development would also be promoted (Table 7.1).

Since the MIDP could not be implemented everywhere in the district simultaneously, only a few areas were selected to be the initial focus of attention, a compromise between the need to concentrate scarce resources to achieve a substantial impact and the need to disperse investments so as to reach a larger beneficiary group. The basic territorial unit of the project was actually the sub-catchment basin, selected because it provided both physical coherence and a population small enough (approximately twenty families) to function as a community. It later proved to be advantageous to base project activities on administrative areas (sub-locations) rather than physical areas.

After lengthy deliberations, the donor agreed that a new autonomous management unit would not be established to administer the project, instead the established ministries would provide the necessary personnel. These ministries would be encouraged to participate actively in the MIDP by cash awards and other incentives. Each participant would retain executive authority, but project activities would be coordinated by a program officer (PMO) responsible to the Ministry of Economic Planning. The PMO would, in turn, be assisted by technical specialists (some expatriate) who would help ensure the steady flow of funds and would perform the critical task of bridging the gaps between ministries. It was understood that some activities (conservation, water) would have to be more closely integrated than others (rural industries).

In order to avoid the familiar pattern of superimposing a program from above, the MIDP was decentralized with most planning taking place at the district level. A District Steering Committee was formed to expedite this process. It included all relevant department heads and the District Commissioner and was charged with establishing links to other district

TABLE 7.1

MIDP Components and Relative Funding Levels

	Phase I (1978-83)	Phase II (1983-86)
1. Crop Development	(14 percent) training, demonstration, pre-extension trials, research	(11 percent) improved extension and better links between extension and research
2. Livestock Development	(17 percent) tick control, stock improvement, dairy, beekeeping, fodder grass improvement	(9 percent) same plus goats and improved administration
3. Soil and Water Conservation	(3 percent) comprehensive soil conservation measures, training, nursery support	included under agriculture
4. Water Development	(37 percent) dam constructions, large scale rural water supply scheme, low technology water scheme	(44 percent) provide basic water supplies in dryer areas for 10 percent of population
5. Forestry	(6 percent) tree planting and nurseries, research	(4 percent) same
6. Cooperative Development	(4 percent) credit supply, stores, training	(12 percent) same plus revolving credit fund, mobile banking and larger stores for wider range of inputs
7. Rural Industry	(2 percent) workshop cluster	(6 percent) same plus loans for entire district

8. Social Services	(2 percent) training, materials and equipment	(5 percent) emphasis on self-help plus functional literacy campaign for 100,000 adults
9. Physical Infrastructure	(2 percent) roads and bridges	
10. Aerial Photography	(2 percent)	
11. Housing	(1 percent)	
12. Economic Planning		(9 percent) improved PMU management and monitoring capacity plus special funds for small projects Development of a model for district focused development elsewhere

Source: Meyer, 1981:7-9 and MIDP, 1983:1.1.

development programs, preparing and supervising the implementation of annual work plans and budgets, and revising, if necessary, ideas submitted by the ministries.[8] Decisions on the dispersement of funds could be made at the district level, allowing for quick and efficient project implementation.

The MIDP staff also realized that the most likely programs to become institutionalized were those based on the active involvement of the local population. With this end in mind, the project organized sub-location seminars at which rural people could ask questions and encouraged local leaders to meet for discussions on their own.[9] Often this group of leaders constituted itself as a Divisional Development Committee, including such members as the chiefs and assistant chiefs, elected officials, organizers of *Mwethya* groups, and church or school activists. The MIDP management considered this type of participation to be a central focus of the program and there is no doubt that local involvement did play a role in fostering appropriate sub-project design and implementation and encouraging self-help activities that were complementary to the MIDP program.

In addition to emphasizing decentralization and participation, the MIDP attempted to combine conservation and production in such a way that the two activities would be mutually reinforcing. Initially, farm credit was only to be made available to farmers who had begun to implement a program of bench terracing and ancillary activities; later this restriction was relaxed as it once again proved difficult to demand that labor be applied to conservation without short-run returns. As a compromise, sub-locations were identified and supplied with a soil conservation supervisor who was to maintain a demonstration project and assist individual farmers over a three-year period. Farmers would then carry out small scale projects on their own fields while the MIDP would continue to be responsible for larger physical works including gully control and drainage. At the same time, strategies for upgrading productivity would gradually be introduced.

One badly eroded catchment can be used to illustrate this process. Its problem was so severe that run-off tended to accumulate in gullies that had gradually become major erosion channels. The arable land in the area had all been terraced but the terraces themselves were in need of repair. The plan for this area called for the application of several techniques including terrace improvement with cut-off drains, tree planting, direct gully control and water harvesting.[10] Farmers in the area have been obligated to fix their terraces and carry out proper tillage and practice manuring and crop rotation. They have also had to avoid overgrazing, attend field days and provide some free labor for building drainage ditches near the road.

The results of the conservation efforts to date have been impressive. The demonstration projects have been widely dispersed through the district so that areas that had been particularly isolated and neglected have received benefits comparable to the more accessible locations. Over 613 Km^2 have been affected by the program compared to a target of 1,000 Km^2.[11] Figure 7.1 shows the distribution of conservation and water supply projects as well as areas added to the Machakos District after independence.

The long-term effectiveness of the MIDP approach will depend in part on the capacity of the soil conservation supervisor to establish a systematic sequence of tasks that can be sustained by sub-divisional committees or another local entity. Land-poor areas are likely to be much more responsive than those where labor is the major constraint. Success will also depend upon the results of related activities designed to promote higher incomes and quality of life and thus justify the ongoing commitment of labor to conservation.

One such activity is the planting of forests in Machakos both for commercial timber production and for watershed protection. Properly managed rural woodlots will not only reduce run-off and improve infiltration rates and water availability to plants but will also be a source of firewood and lumber supplies. Logistical problems have slowed the replanting effort to date but this could become a critical component of the larger program.

Closely associated with conservation is control of the surface flow of water and its delivery to a dispersed rural population. The MIDP has made water supply a priority using a range of strategies that include surface and subsurface earth dams, as well as small projects that tap rock and spring catchments. These efforts have been supplemented by a not insubstantial effort on the part of self-help groups. Some financing has come from the MIDP, but most support has been provided by the Rural Development Fund, a support program for local initiatives that represents the mid 1970s merger of earlier, less effective programs. Between 1974-5 and 1982, at least 72 water supply projects of this type were completed.[12]

The MIDP had initially planned to provide reasonably accessible water supplies for the domestic, livestock, and minor irrigation needs of the rural population of semi-arid Machakos. Although the exact position of dams and small water projects was not specified in the program description, most of the sites were to be located along seasonal streams in the dryer areas. This strategy was modified, however, when it became clear that variable rainfall and high sedimentation rates at these sites were leading to low or unreliable water yields. A new plan was substituted at this point whereby some dams would be built in the hills and then connected to downslope areas by a system of pipes. Another program change was the reduction of small dams to be constructed in Phase I from 55 to 20 and the number of small water projects from 200 to 115. These modifications caused some dissatisfaction in communities that were anticipating reliable water supplies,

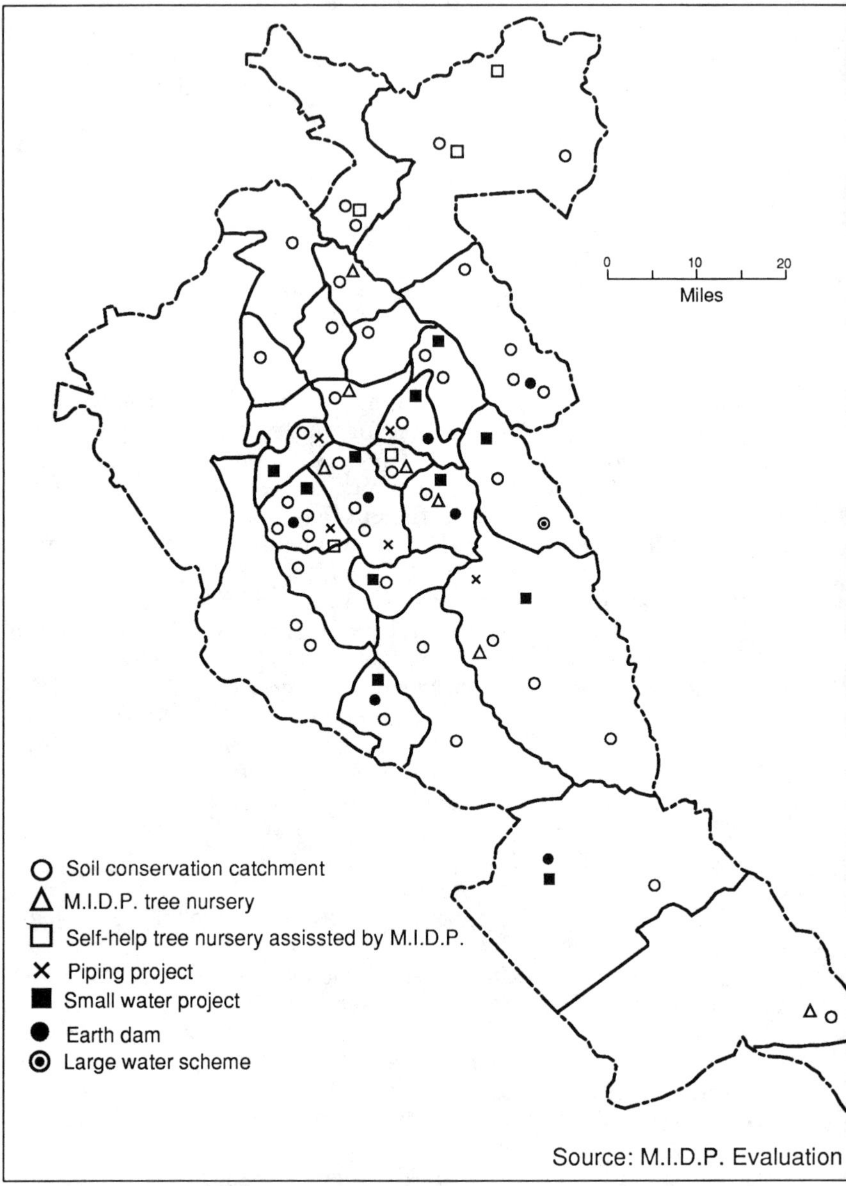

Figure 7.1 MIDP Conservation Activities and Water Prijects

especially since budgetary problems also slowed down the construction of piping systems.

As of the early 1980s distribution of projects was follows: (Figure 7.1):

1) In the highlands three dams were close to completion (one in Mbooni and two in Kalama) with a second in Mbooni not far behind.

2) In the lowlands a few dams were being built in areas that were considered too remote to receive piped water: one in Kisau, one in Muthetheni, and two in Yatta. Two others, including one in Mbitini, had been started. Attempts had also been made to associate small dam projects with demonstration conservation projects whenever possible. These efforts were meant to accomplish two goals: to curtail erosion once run-off was reduced and to provide the incentive of water availability to participants in erosion control program.

As of 1986, more than 105 small projects other than the surface earthen dams had been completed. They were distributed more widely than the earth dams and were thus more accessible to the dispersed lowland population (Table 7.2 and 7.3). One additional large scale project has been designed to serve 16,000 persons in the lowlands of Kibauoni.

As in the case of conservation programs, water supply projects have been planned to include a high level of participation. The MIDP has supported the formation of *Mwethya* groups, reinforcing continuity with the past when mutual assistance played an important role in surviving drought and carrying out community based tasks.[13] Local participation has also encouraged by soliciting the input of farmers and leaders before sites are selected for possible development. The evaluation of watershed, for technical feasibility, size of benefit group, and local water need, has only been carried out after it is clear that the applicant community has the potential to form a water committee that can be charged with some responsibilities.[14]

It is not yet been determined what role voluntary labor can play in support of rural-based projects. A flow of resources in an area can be a powerful impetus to self-help but it is most effective in the highlands where high population densities and relative wealth facilitate the sharing of labor and/or capital cost. In poor areas, self-help activities can easily be undermined because the political leadership is limited in size and experience, because farmers have little education or because of severe labor constraints.[15] In the long-run it is probably not feasible to rely on voluntary committees to carry out such tasks as the maintenance of water projects. When this approach was tried in the past in Machakos district, the result was gradual damage to dams including widespread siltation. Maintenance tasks are

TABLE 7.2

Summary of Small Project Data

Location	Number of Projects	Total Population Served	Total Cost (Ksh '000)
Kalama	23	9,150	1,440
Mbooni	4	6,825	2,110
Muvuti	4	6,200	1,200
Kisau	17	7,030	835
Wamunyu	16	7,725	960
Okia	1	120	85
Kibauni	14	3,700	685
Muthetheni	6	1,520	217
Makueni	12	2,300	1,290
Kathonzweni	5	1,550	230
Mitaboni	1	n.a.	n.a.
Total	102	46,200	9,052

Source: Table 11.5, p. 11.8, MIDP Evaluation.

TABLE 7.3

Estimated Population to be Served by MIDP Water Projects (Phase I)

Section		Population
Earth dams (excluding Yatta Division)		51,000
Earth dams (Yatta Division)		15,500
Small water projects		47,500
	Subtotal	114,000
Large water supply (Kibauni)		16,000
	Total	130,000

Source: Table 11.6, p. 11.9, MIDP Evaluation.

probably better assigned to appropriate local government authorities (which often need to be revived in Kenya) while *Mwethya*-type groups should concentrate on construction and on regulating the use of new facilities so as not to exacerbate normal wear and tear.

Complementing the MIDP effort at conservation and water control has been the promotion of improved crop productivity. This component was designed to raise incomes and purchasing power which would in turn provide an economic base for expanded rural services and infrastructure. The MIDP hoped to generate an additional KSH 23 million in participant income though such mechanisms as farm credit, new crops and technologies, crop security, and improved marketing and input provision.[16] These gains were then expected to encourage farmers to invest labor and capital in preserving the vulnerable resource base of the region.

The goal of higher productivity has been supported by both project and non-project activities. In 1977, for example, USAID collaborated with FAO in researching crops and organizational strategies that could be used in the ASALs. The International Institute for Tropical Agriculture (IITA), which had been established in part to deal with semi-arid Africa, was tapped to provide research findings, particularly with regard to crops and technologies within the reach of a typical smallholder.

The MIDP also built on earlier efforts by the Ministry of Agriculture. In 1976 a project was launched that provided credit for a specific combination of food and cash crops rather than for cash crops alone. Ideally, participating farmers were to grow designated crops on approximately three acres (two acres for a food crop and one for a so-called anchor crop that could readily be marketed). Credit was to be used primarily for hybrid seed purchases, land preparation, and weeding costs. Fertilizer supplies were sometimes made available but under another program which had established a stabilization fund to avoid the need for heavy fertilizer subsidies.[17]

The MIDP incorporated parts of this earlier project but with some basic design changes. Loan default had already become a problem in several cash crop credit programs, in part because of a dearth of well-trained cooperative officers. The MIDP approach to this problem was to institute staff training and to create sub-locational credit committees that would help supervise loan repayments. Another change was meant to correct the familiar problem of insufficient transport and storage facilities for inputs and marketed goods. The MIDP emphasized marketing services fairly early in the program cycle so that by 1982 there were twenty-two new storage facilities planned--and local cooperative societies were being encouraged.

There was one problem for which MIDP did not have an immediate strategy. The food-crop, cash-crop and credit combination had originally been designed for the high potential areas. As early as 1977 the EEC seemed aware of the potential difficulty of applying the program to the ASALs, particularly in terms of the impact of unreliable rainfall on loan repayment schedules. The project management could only hope that crop and technology packages would make the program economically feasible.

The first step in this direction was the selection of such drought resistant crops as sunflower and cotton in some combination with beans and Katumani maize. Secondly, appropriate technologies were examined, the most promising of which was the multi-purpose tool bar. This device was supposed to be an improvement over the simple moldboard plow in that it could break up the ground before the arrival of the rains (allowing earlier planting) and could be used for weeding operations. In 1979, 450 units were made available on credit, with the idea that they would be particularly useful in the more remote areas of Machakos where fields were larger.[18] At the same time farmers were being urged to adopt improved maize cribs for on-farm storage. The cribs had been produced by local craftsmen to provide better ventilation and thus cut down on fungus development.

Another important part of the productivity initiative was the improvement of extension services and the provision of farmer training. MIDP added crop and farm management specialists as well as extra extension staff and vehicles to existing extension staff of the Ministry of Agriculture (MOA). The crop specialists were given the task of using the MOA structure to bring about the diffusion of "proven methods of dryland farming through farmer training, crop demonstrations, and pre-extension trials."[19] In 1982-83, for example, the MIDP used leaflets in the Kamba language as part of two-day training programs for more than 6,000 farmers. The courses covered food crops (maize beans, pigeon peas, and cow peas), soil conservation, livestock, and credit. Demonstrations were organized on one acre plots belonging to over 100 farmers.

The mainstay of the commercial part of the program came to be cotton. This crop had first been introduced to Machakos District before independence and then abandoned because neither the total output nor the per hectare yields justified establishing costly production and marketing-related infrastructure. Cotton continued to be grown in selected areas of Kenya but output stagnated until the mid-1970's when substantial price increases and a credit scheme were introduced.[20] Promotional efforts were gradually extended to Machakos District and similar areas which had previously rejected cotton as a cash crop and it was here that production increases were the most dramatic.

After a period of initial growth, production of cotton began to fluctuate in response to problems of bad weather or logistics. At this point the MIDP was able to intervene, particularly in terms of the marketing environment.

First the cotton cooperative received an interest-free loan to cover the cost of five lorries and ten containers, each with a capacity of nine tons. This was followed by the establishment of an innovative radio-controlled collection system that by 1981 was able to pick up 5,000 tons of raw cotton from 300 buying points. In the same year at least half of the Machakos cotton could finally be delivered to a new ginery at Makueni rather than having to be carried the longer distance to the ginery at Kitui.

A word should be said here about efforts being made in livestock management and related activities. The MIDP included a component which called for increases in marketed cattle (50% in two years), control of tick-borne diseases, and a doubling of milk production in the district. Two veterinary officers and eight technical officers were made available to the program to further this goal. However, few changes have been documented as a result of MIDP activities, and the program emphasis has started to shift to dairying.

One final area in which changes have been taken place is that of urban services. The Machakos Regional Plan provided the basic guidelines, leaving the MIDP in a peripheral role except for those services most directly related to improved agricultural production. The most impressive change has been the increased number of primary schools. Technically, each local center with a catchment population of approximately 5-6,000 was to have primary school, but schools have emerged wherever local groups exerted pressure on government or carried out self-help activities.[21] In inaccessible, sparsely populated areas stimulating self-help groups has been much more difficult as participants have had to develop a site that might be more than 8 km from any given homestead.

Secondary school education has also becoming more widely available although the emphasis in Kenya has changed to improving the quality of existing facilities rather than building new ones. Resources were to be used to upgrade schools with few well-trained teachers or a narrow range of offerings but in Machakos District, where approximately fifteen percent of the children of secondary school age have been enrolled, pressure has continued to build new school facilities. The overall pattern of secondary school distribution in the district has come to conform fairly well to the regional plan although there is some tributary areas overlap and not every school has been located in a designated market center.[22] Most encouraging, each of the four lowland and intermediate locations which had no post-primary education at the time of the original plan has acquired at least one.

Two other educational programs have not yet reached an advanced stage of implementation. One of these (village polytechnics) will be discussed subsequently. The second program has promoted adult literacy and has been particularly useful in remote areas where literacy skills were often the key variable after security in the adoption of agricultural innovations.[23]

Health services have also been expanded but they have remained predominantly curative, with only twelve percent of the 1982 annual budget going directly to rural health facilities. In spite of rhetoric to the contrary, trained medical personnel have continued to be concentrated in the largest cities and rural health services have reached only half of the rural population of Kenya as a whole. In the Eastern Province of Kenya the access situation remains very poor but within the old boundaries of Machakos District, almost the whole population is finally within eight kilometers of a facility, a minimum goal of the Department of Health.

The specific location of health facilities has not changed much from the pattern prevailing in 1976 (Table 6.10). Among the new additions have been a hospital in Kangundo, (H), a new health center in Makueni (L) and new dispensaries in Kilungu (H), Muthetheni (L), and Kibauoni (L). There are funds being earmarked for a hospital in Mbooni (H), Kilungu (H) and Makueni (L), but also plans for a denser network of facilities in underserved areas. Ideally, a health facility will become available for every 50,000 persons, which in turn implies a dispensary for each local center and a health center for each market center. To date, most facilities in Machakos District can be found in designated locations.

2. Continuity and Change

By the mid-1970s the Government of Kenya had begun to make basic changes in its rural development policies. In the decade since these decisions were made it has become clear that much has been accomplished but that some issues remain intractable. The government is rectifying earlier mistakes but can neither undo all the damage of the past nor readily cope with continued rapid population growth. The current situation can best be understood by examining five major themes: a) the incorporation of natural resource management into crop production planning, b) the current status of the traditional Kamba modes of adjustment, c) relative regional equity, d) decentralization and e) agricultural productivity in the ASALs.

a. The Role of Natural Resource Management

The problems of highland erosion and the deterioration of semi-arid areas under pressure from human and livestock population growth have been a focus of attention for decades. Unfortunately, these problems were initially dealt with in a heavy-handed manner by central government bureaucrats who were insensitive to local needs. Many programs designed to ameliorate the impact of drought generated as much resentment as cooperation. Yet, in spite of numerous counter-productive efforts, the colonial approach to resource management did ultimately result in widespread acceptance of terracing, dam building, and the use of *Mwethya*-type self-help groups.

The cessation of conservation programs in many areas following independence created new problems that were exacerbated by a high population growth rate and the migration of people and animals into the lowlands.[24] This situation focused attention on land preservation and finally led to the decision that any projects in the ASALs would make local resource management their core activity. This position has been reinforced by recent studies of the African food problem including one which states explicitly that "Africa needs programs based on environmental goals not on rates of return."[25]

When measured against these concerns, the MIDP is in many ways a prototype program. It has incorporated the concept of conservation across the board and has proved the feasibility of combining group-based conservation activities and the expansion of water supplies.[26] The project has also evaluated alternative sites for water storage, providing comparative data on lowland reservoirs versus highland sites combined with piped delivery downslope.

One of the more exciting areas of experimentation has been the use of agroforestry to reduce runoff, supply fodder, and provide enough firewood to substitute for manure or crop residues as cooking fuel. The MIDP staff has already planted 500 acres of protection forest, expanded its nursery component, and provided seedlings and technical advice to self-help groups and individuals willing to establish an agroforestry unit. The focus of attention should gradually shift to alley cropping: the combination of leguminous shrubs like lucena (or acacia in the dryer areas) with selected crops.[27]

Before the conservation component can be labeled a success, an important question still has to be answered: can the program be continued once MIDP funding has been phased out? Certainly those innovations that are more costly or more demanding of technical assistance will be the most difficult to sustain or to emulate. The project needs to emphasize the more affordable approaches that depend mainly on local skills and resources such as the use of crop residues to maintain soil stability and the building of small stone walls along contours to insure that rainfall is spread over a wide area. Both the application of residues and water spreading techniques improve moisture penetration and in some cases obviate the need for additional water control projects. Other approaches require only inexpensive materials or technologies from outside the district such as the dissemination of small clay stoves that reduce fuelwood requirements.

Even if the cost of conservation can be reduced in a post-MIDP era, a second question remains: will farmers in the semi-arid areas be willing to keep up their efforts at protecting the environment if they are not able to augment their income through increased productivity or off-farm employment? Certainly conservation and production will have to be planned jointly in the future since neither focus is adequate by itself. This issue will be addressed further under theme 5.

b. Traditional Kamba modes of Adjustment

In the planning and implementation of such programs as the MIDP the Kenyan government has come to recognize the importance of traditional survival strategies including mutual assistance, diversification, and mobility. These strategies have been incorporated into new programs whenever possible particularly in the lowlands where they are critical to the improvement of current conditions.

The theme of diversification has always been particularly important in Machakos District and this strategy is now vital to the area's economy. Today, most rural families are engaged in several productive activities, even if on a very small scale. These include cultivating one or more cash crops, raising livestock for sale, engaging in handicraft production, selling rope, clay pots, charcoal or firewood, and earning money from off-farm employment. This range of potential income sources has been credited with lowering levels of protein-energy malnutrition (PEM) among Kamba children during what would normally be considered the hungry period of the year before crops have been harvested.[28] Multiple income sources have also provided resources for investment in land, inputs, equipment, or animals. In effect, willingness to become involved in a development project or to carry out agricultural innovations often reflects the degree to which a family has alternatives to fall back on.

The government has come to view the economy of Machakos District as one in which the combination of farming and off-farm activities is critical to augmenting incomes and increasing security. With this perspective in mind, policy decisions have been made to supplement the initiatives of rural households and take an active role in employment generation. Efforts have begun to build factories in areas outside of Nairobi and Mombasa, although industry still remains concentrated in the two major cities.[29] The pattern of concentration even carries over to the informal sector which also requires access to supplies, infrastructure, and markets.[30]

More success has been achieved in dispersing small scale industry through the mechanism of the Craft Training Center (CTC) previously known as the village polytechnic. This approach grew out of the efforts of the NCCK (National Council of Churches in Kenya) to decrease high rates of rural-urban migration. The program which finally emerged after several years of experimentation was based on the combination of training for school leavers and close links to local shops at which students could obtain contract work.[31]

The MIDP developed its own employment oriented component which was designed for but not limited to graduates of village polytechnics. Rural workplaces were established, each of which distributed loans to entrepreneurs to cover the cost of equipment purchases. These expenditures have been kept to a minimum by the use of appropriate technology.[32] In the second phase of the project the rural workplace component will include one additional workplace with a revolving loan fund that will serve the entire district.[33]

The rural workshops represent the major MIDP effort in the area of household income generation but there have been other projects such as beekeeping, dairying, and poultry raising. Beekeeping has expanded to include 27,000 participants but it is dairy that has been emphasized in Phase II with technical assistance in calf breeding, stall feeding, and forage development.[34] Women's groups have also received increasing attention, especially those which have established small businesses based on poultry, vegetables, or handicrafts. Hopefully, new skills can be introduced to replace those which have died out. At the very least, the MIDP and related activities can overcome the most serious constraints on local enterprises by providing loans and/or materials.

These diverse programs have been distributed in such a way as to emphasize district-wide coverage. As might be expected, most successes have been experienced in the highlands where income and population levels can support more off-farm employment. Craft centers and other projects in the lowlands will probably continue to suffer from limited demand until agricultural productivity and thus local purchasing power increases.

The expansion of rural enterprise has been particularly important to the component of the rural population (possibly forty percent in the highlands and more in the lowlands) that can be classified as low income smallholders.[35] Such households have usually experienced land or other critical resource constraints that will probably worsen in the future. Since these families are more likely to evolve into a landless or land poor rural proletariat then into successful commercial farmers, income generating opportunities are required to stave off endemic poverty.

The diversification strategy has become inextricably linked with the mobility strategy which continues to include the option of a satellite farm. One study of 104 households in northern Machakos (predominantly highland) found that 52% of the sample operated a farm in a second location.[36] Actual migration, however, no longer implies finding unclaimed land on a frontier, rather it is linked to employment that is seasonal, annual, or long- term. Household mobility is often circular in nature, as can be seen by examining some of the rural-urban connections that might develop within a hypothetical life cycle:

1) Children may spend several years outside of their family homestead, a phenomenon that was once associated with protection against drought but which now provides opportunities for education or apprenticeships. The distribution of children also reflects social norms whereby older women take care of the children of relatives, in part as an investment in that child's future.

2) After completing primary or secondary school or an alternative training program such children may become urban residents but they are not at that point necessarily isolated from their rural villages. Town dwellers who are employed are expected to provide financial assistance to rural relatives. The contribution of migrant labor to rural household income can be as much as 50%.[37] According to one evaluation, even low and middle income urban migrants can be counted on to remit at least 21% of their income back to rural areas for such purposes as school fees, taxes, investment in land or rural business.[38]

3) When urban dwellers become unemployed or retire they can return to their villages and resume a rural life. The skills and income they have acquired can then be used more directly to invest in a farm or off-farm enterprise. Savings can also be applied to a rural relative's education and so begin the cycle again. It is a positive attribute of the Kenyan economy and society that rural-urban ties of this type are still strong and function to moderate what would otherwise be substantial rural-urban income differentials.

c. Relative Regional Equity

The initial post independence period in Kenya was characterized by the rapid expansion of cash crop cultivation by Africans and by a concomitant increase in the average income of smallholders. The growth spurt was facilitated by the availability of land for resettlement and some constructive government policies. Subsequently, these conditions have given way to several years of drought, rapid population growth, and land scarcity. It is no longer possible to hide the problems and inequities that were disguised by the favorable economic statistics of the mid 1960's to early 1970's. The government is now faced with problems that have exacerbated inequities both within and between regions.

The discrepancy between highland and lowland regions in Kenya, particularly in Machakos District, has been discussed at length and traced to its origins during the early colonial period. The government continued to ignore the detrimental impact of its policies on lowland agriculture until disaster threatened.[39] It was the mid 1970s before a commitment was finally made to rectify this type of inequity and it is necessary to examine what has happened since.

On the positive side, investments have been made in rural services and infrastructure as well as in research on cash crops and technologies appropriate to the ASALs. These and other changes have had an impact; on a Kenya-wide scale it can be shown that from 1948 to the present inter-regional inequality of income has steadily declined.[40] In Machakos itself the MIDP has been able to direct substantial resources to the ASALs resulting in improved access to water, employment, storage, marketing and other services, extension and resource management.

On the negative side, some sources of inequity are more difficult to correct including, of course, the basic differences in physical environment. There is still social and political inequity as well. For example, the Machakos Union which oversees the cash crop marketing societies in the district has been diverting inputs, revenues, and vehicles to the highland coffee societies. In exchange, they have allegedly agreed to have the more experienced societies train personnel from the young and struggling coops in the semi-arid areas.[41] At another scale, the selection of rural development project areas across Kenya still seems to reflect the distribution of political influence; a factor that correlates strongly with wealth and population density.[42]

One of the major sources of highland/lowland inequality in the past has been the availability of urban services and there has been some success making such services more widely available. Secondary cities and towns are growing faster than before 1970. Yet, government investment as part of the growth center strategy has lagged behind targets and available resources are still concentrated in the largest towns.[43] It is now widely accepted that the growth center strategy was initially too ambitious, especially in terms of coverage. Furthermore, the program has not been flexible enough to accommodate unanticipated changes such as rapidly growing towns that were not included in the original plan or designated towns that have fallen behind predicted rates of growth.

As for the services themselves, the trend has been favorable for some but not for others. As early as the 1950's the government began to acknowledge that lowland locations were poorly served with health and educational facilities. Plans were made to assist in the building and staffing of lowland schools and dispensaries, especially in response to self-help initiatives. Almost every location in the original district now has both a dispensary and a secondary school while the ratio of population to primary schools has come close to the figures for the highlands. Yet, with regard to extension services, studies in areas similar to Machakos District have shown that the farmers with the best land and largest farms were three to four times more likely to be contacted by an agricultural agent and that the extension effort to date had widened the gap between rich and poor farmers.[33]

The provision of services is also hampered by inadequate linkages between highlands and lowlands. The number of good quality roads and regular bus and lorry routes is insufficient to maintain reliable contact throughout the annual crop cycle. The MIDP and other projects should probably have included fewer site-specific programs and made more of an effort to enhance flows of goods and services along the altitudinal continuum.[45]

Part of the difficulty involved in reversing the general concentration of resources and attention in the medium to high potential areas is the government's reluctance to jeopardize the yields that have been achieved in the highlands, a perspective that was reinforced when food shortages and other economic problems surfaced after 1978. Even the foreign aid donors that acknowledge the need for research and interventions in the low lying areas still recommend that a major portion of their assistance be highlands oriented.[46] Both donors and government are responding to the 1) the potential for even higher productivity in the hills with additional infrastructure, marketing services, and improved technologies, and 2) the high density of population that remains in these areas in spite of substantial outmigration.[47] The split in rural development goals has meant that in spite of the rhetoric to the contrary, there are still biases in resource allocation that continue to undermine lowland economic growth.

d. Decentralization

In many ways the MIDP provided the ideal example of decentralization when the government decided to deemphasize the top-down approaches to rural development. The 1984-88 plan introduced the "District Focus for Rural Development" which was meant to spread some of the guiding principals of the MIDP to the rest of the country and to make the district the basic planning unit.

The key entity in this new system, the District Development Committee (DDC), has a similar structure to its counterpart in Machakos. Reporting to the DDCs are the Divisional Development Committees which reach down to local organizations and leaders. This structure calls for greater cooperation between ministries and the upgrading of ministry staff in each district so that the additional responsibilities will be handled effectively.

The new system also results in less discretion on the part of the ministry in allocating its budget. The AIE (authority to incur expenditures) remains with the ministry but can be exercised at the district level. Furthermore, approximately ten percent of a ministry's budget has to be committed to district specific projects. Support for such projects can come from several sources (the line ministries, self-help activities, local authorities and special program funds) but in each case the DDC sets priorities and coordinates investments.[48]

For the district focus to be successful it will have to do more than transfer decisions from a national to a regional bureaucracy; it will actually have to transfer some of the central government's power to the local level. So far it would seem that the DDC remains too closely tied to the national bureaucracy and that local participation decision making is still marginal.[49] Even the capacity of district level officers to allocate funds directly has not always changed their orientation from the ministerial headquarters in Nairobi to the rural population they are expected to serve.

Several other problems remain. The only forum for direct popular expression, the *baraza* or local meeting, seems more geared to giving district leaders a forum than to providing local groups with an opportunity to air their grievances or suggest policy.[50] Women's organizations and other entities that represent the different interest groups at the community level are not also effectively linked to the decisions being made by the DDC. Finally, in those districts which resemble Machakos in having considerable internal ecological variation, the old pattern of national government favoritism toward the better-endowed areas can be replicated at the district level.[51]

e. Agricultural Productivity in the ASALs

Integrated rural development in Machakos District was supposed to promote the absorption of the semi-arid areas into the national economy. This was an ambitious goal given decades of neglect and a high level of deprivation and was probably overly optimistic. Some basic difficulties still remain and new approaches are being devised to deal with them.

The most important of the conundrums has been the persistence of low levels of agricultural productivity and the lack of any promising technology that could change the situation in the near future. According to one analysis, "agricultural science simply does not yet offer the subsistence farmer in semi-arid conditions as much as it does the farmers with an abundance of water at their disposal."[52] Even when fertilizers are available they may be only marginally effective since crops react much more dramatically to mineral supplements in humid areas then they do in areas of moisture shortfall.

A major deficit has been the dearth of hybrid varieties of lowland crops (Katumani maize being an exception) because past research focused on humid areas.[53] At the agricultural research center in Nigeria (IITA), progress is finally being made in developing improved strains of sorghum, pigeon peas, cow peas, and early maturing maize although not much has yet been accomplished with millet. Furthermore, a strain of sorghum that is resistant to the parasite striga has begun to be made available to farmers.[54]

Not only is there a lack of innovations that would dramatically increase production in the ASALs but the issue of access is most critical in these areas. It has proven difficult to provide credit, fertilizer, or other inputs at the appropriate time: the private sector has avoided or overcharged remote areas while the public sector has been inefficient. The same can be said about marketing. According to one theory, dryland farmers and herders will be reluctant to innovate until they have a cash crop that can provide them with security, yet the successful marketing of such a crop remains problematical in the ASALs.[55]

The MIDP has encountered all of the problems described above in its efforts to increase the productivity of agriculture in the semi-arid areas of Machakos District. It has proved cumbersome to supervise the extension staff in the more remote areas at the same time that extension officers have been frustrated in trying to coordinate widely dispersed farmers. As a result, field days and crop demonstrations have had to be reduced in quantity and scale. Nor has the veterinary staff been able to cover its extensive territory, in part because of vehicular breakdowns.

The few technological innovations that have been introduced by the MIDP have not been as popular as expected for several reasons. Adoption of the multi-service tool bar, for example, has been slow, the result of initial malfunctions and a general reluctance on the part of farmers to give up their traditional plows. Even the improved maize cribs have been rejected by a majority of farmers who are unwilling to substitute for their old storage cribs. These conservative reactions are indicative of both a dearth of reliable income sources and environmental uncertainty with its need for risk avoidance. The major cash crop in the lowlands, cotton, is subject to wide price fluctuations and has not yet yielded enough income to produce real security.

Given the lack of easy answers to the problems of the ASALs, the only option open would seem to be to follow the recommendations made for natural resource management (and discussed in chapter one) to put less emphasis on outside inputs and more on improvements that can be generated with local resources. For example, research and field testing could be focused on varieties that do particularly well in the mixed stands which are so common among smallholders. It has already been shown that an intercrop of selected millets and sorghums can provide a combined yield that is 25 percent greater than if the crops had been grown separately while the figure was 51 percent for a millet/cowpeas intercrop.[57]

Also important is encouraging the production increases that can be expected from combinations of early planting and proper spacing and tillage. The MIDP, at least in the short run, will have to concentrate on this type of pragmatic measure to improve productivity even if the end results only provide marginal improvements. It is probably also necessary to plan on just one modification of the production system at a time in keeping with local preferences.[58] In any case, there is no substitute for the as yet unavailable appropriate technology or hybrid crop that could dramatically improve the potential of the typical ASAL farm household.

f. Final overview

When we look at the economic situation in Africa today it continues to appear grim. Some of the basic causes are beyond local control. The poor performance of exports, to include a decline in some countries of fifty percent in export earnings since 1980, reflects competition from other sources of raw materials and from synthetic substitutes. Low export prices contribute in turn to a shortage of capital that has not been alleviated by either international assistance programs or such private sources as banks.

The worsening state of external conditions has been accompanied in most African countries by an ongoing slide in agricultural productivity. This stagnation has been blamed on many factors including environmental crises, meager profits for farmers, and logistical problems. In fact, many governments have been raising the share of cash crop revenue that accrues to farmers, but this improvement has been offset by the decreasing world commodity prices. Farmers who produce for an internal market remain under threat from a potentially volatile and constantly growing urban population that resents any increase in the costs of foodstuffs. As for logistical problems, they reflect foreign exchange constraints that make it difficult to obtain the fuel and spare parts to keep produce flowing toward the market or inputs moving toward the farm. Extension and similar services have also been cut back as governments have reduced expenditures in compliance with IMF requirements.

Since these larger issues seem intractable when viewed in terms of the continent as a whole they need to be reduced in scale to the context of a single region. This study has tried to provide a micro-level analysis: a detailed examination of the relationship between economic performers and the long-term processes transpiring in a selected areas. The specific example in this case, the Kamba of Machakos District, developed an extremely flexible and multi-faceted approach to production under semi-arid conditions.

The colonial regime that was established in the region introduced an alternative structure that was more rigid, less environmentally sensitive and more conducive to both social and regional stratification.

The perspective of historical geography has been used to show how, at each stage of the evolving relationship between the Kamba and the British colonial administration, the local population struggled to maintain its system of survival. The first adaptation to be threatened was the mobility strategy, undermined by forced removals and the establishment of boundaries. By the 1930s, mutual assistance and the use of rituals had become less important and linkages between highlands and lowlands were beginning to weaken. Eventually, only one strategy remained significant: the development of alternative activities, first in response to drought but later as a compensation for land shortages and other factors. At the same time that the colonial regime was undermining all of these components of the local survival system, it was also changing the local spatial structure. Established focal points of activity and patterns of movement were ignored in favor of those areas that were relevant to colonial priorities, usually potential sites for commercial agriculture or mining. This pattern was reinforced by investments in agriculture, transport and selected central places.

Post World War II political and economic realities dictated that the colonial administration would finally attempt to reach out, both in terms of expanding its spatial structure and improving productivity on African farms. In Machakos, the spatial initiatives involved the first efforts to incorporate the lowlands, initially through the provision of basic services, then with environmental and agricultural programs and infrastructure. Some of these new programs were innovative but they often couldn't overcome the mistrust that was a legacy of earlier, more manipulative efforts. When an independent African state was finally created in Kenya, it perpetuated the colonial pattern, continuing to use the technological "quick-fix" to deal with complex issues.

The culmination of this study occurs when the collective wisdom of the local inhabitants begins to be accepted by the state administration. Today, there is finally emerging a new appreciation of small-scale, low-cost interventions, suitable to particular settings and reflecting "indigenous structures and designs.[59] This is especially true when the interventions are compatible with mixed-cropping systems and are based on at least some recycling of organic material. Given the current unfavorable world economic climate, the rate of population growth in Africa, and the lack of any technical intervention that can rapidly raise the productivity of the average smallholder in areas like Machakos, there is no choice but to tap local knowledge and institutions in working toward a more sustainable relationship between people and resources.

CHAPTER 7 - REFERENCES

[1] USAID, Palmer et al., Kenya Pre-Investment Invetory, 17.

[2] Murdock, *The Poverty of Nations*, 304.

[3] Dickson, "Heavy Emphasis on Agriculture," *Financial Times*, June, 1978, 21-23.

[4] United Nations, International Labor Organization (ILO), "Employment, Incomes, and Equality in Kenya."

[5] Government of Kenya (GOK), *Kenya Development Plan*, 1974-78, 134.

[6] GOK, Machakos Integrated Development Program (MIDP), "Brief for the Minister of Cooperative Development," 1.

[7] GOK, MIDP, "Submission to the European Community," 2-4.

[8] GOK, MIDP, "Brief for the Minister of Cooperative Development," 2.

[9] GOK, Overseas Development Institute, "MIDP Evaluation," 5.12.

[10] GOK, MIDP, "Concise Plan for Kyangala Catchment," 2.

[11] GOK, Overseas Development Institute, "MIDP Evaluation," 9.11.

[12] Ibid., 11.1.

[13] Ford, "Local Leadership in Resource Planning," 12.

[14] USAID, Meyer, "Organization of Rural Development," 26.

[15] Holmquist, "Self-Help," 79.

[16] GOK, Overseas Development Institute, "MIDP Evaluation," 6.1.

[17] DeWilde, *Experience with Agricultural Development*, 15.

[18] GOK, Overseas Development Institute, "MIDP Evaluation," 7.7.

[19] Ibid., 6.4.

[20] DeWilde, *Experience with Agricultural Development*, 22.

[21] GOK, Ministry of Land and Settlement, *Human Settlements*, 154.

[22] Ibid., 156.

[23] USAID, Fleuret, "Kenya Social and Institutional Profile," 204.

[24] Ibid., 22.

[25] Brown and Wolf, *Reversing Africa's Decline*, 66.

[26] GOK, MIDP, "Project Dossier," 2.5.

[27] Brown and Wolf, *Reversing Africa's Decline*, 47.

[28] Onchere and Sloof, "Nutrition and Disease in Machakos," 44.

[29] Mbogua, "A Strategy for Town Development in Kenya," 7-8.

[30] USAID, Fleuret, "Kenya Social and Institutional Profile," 120.

[31] Barker and Ferguson, "The Craft Training Center in Kenya," 75.

[32] GOK, Overseas Development Institute, "MIDP Evaluation," 14:6.

[33] GOK, MIDP, "Submission to the European Community," 45.

[34] GOK, MIDP, "Project Dossier," 44.

[35] USAID, Fleuret, "Kenya Social and Institutional Profile," 18.

[36] Van Ginneken et al., "Mobility Patterns in Machakos District," 88.

[37] Ibid., 90.

[38] USAID, Fleuret, "Kenya Social and Institutional Profile," 30.

[39] Yaeger, *Africa's Conservation for Development*, 17.

[40] Carlson, *Economic and Social Transformation*, 51.

[41] GOK, Overseas Development Institute, "MIDP Evaluation," 6.

[42] Oyugi, "Center-Periphery Relations," 154.

[43] Mbogua, "A Strategy for Town Development in Kenya," 7.

[44] House and Killick, "Social Justice in Kenya's Rural Development," 54.

[45] Bernard, "Planning in the Kenya Drylands," 69.

[46] USAID, "Country Development Strategy Statement (CDSS) for Kenya," 1985.

[47] House and Killick, "Social Justice in Kenya's Rural Development," 54.

[48] GOK, MIDP, "Annual Work Plan," 1984-86.

[49] Mackenzie and Taylor, "Regional and Rural Devleopment," 3.

[50] Ibid., 23.

[51] Bernard, "Planning in the Kenya Drylands," 68.

[52] Brown and Wolf, *Reversing Africa's Decline*, 65.

[53] Timberlake, *Africa in Crisis*, 147.

[54] Harrison, *The Greening of Africa*, 103.

[55] USAID, Fleuret, "Kenya Social and Institutional Profile," 96.

[56] Harrison, *The Greening of Africa*, 109.

[57] Eicher, *Transforming African Agriculture*, 16.

[58] Callaghy, "Debt and Structural Adjustments in Africa," 18.

BIBLIOGRAPHY

I. Primary Sources

A. Kenya National Archives

1. Machakos District *Annual Reports*, 1907-62.
2. Machakos District *Political Record Book*, 1909-38.
3. Machakos District *Handing Over Notes*, 1949-60.
4. *Kenya Native Affairs Reports*, 1929-32, 1933-35, and 1936-38.
5. Machakos District *Monthly Intelligence Reports*, 1945-50.
6. Machakos District, Department of Agriculture, *Annual Reports*: 1932-54, 1955-58, 1962-64, 1966, 69, and 1970-72.
7. African Land Development (ALDEV) *Annual Reports*, 1945-55.

B. Colonial Office, Departmental, and other Official Government Reports

1. Kenya Colony

1908 Hildebrandt, I. M. "Ethnographic Notes on the Wakamba."

1911 _________. "Papers on Early Machakos History."

1924 Harrison, Rupert. "Report on Efforts to Stimulate Native Production."

1930 Gracie, D. S. "A Preliminary Survey of Some of the Soils of Kenya."

1930's Logan, W. E. M. "Memorandum on Forest Reservations in Machakos Native Reserve."

1933 Kenya Land Commission. "Evidence and Memoranda." (3 volumes).

1937 Barnes, R. 0. "Memorandum on Soil Erosion - Ukamba Reserve."

1937 Maher, C. "Soil Erosion and Land Utilization in the Ukamba Reserve."

1945 Lambert, H. E. "A Note on Native Land Problems in Machakos District With Particular Reference to Reconditioning."

1945 "Machakos Reserve: Facts and Figures."

1945 Logan, W. E. M. "Memorandum on the Forest Reserve in the Machakos Native Reserve."

1945 Musa, A. "Farming in Upper Reaches of Machakos."

1953 Brown, L. H. *The Agricultural Problems and Potentials of the African Lands of Kenya.*

1955 Colonial Office. *East African Royal Commission Report*. London.

1955 Swynnerton, R. J. M. *A Plan to Intensify the Development of African Agriculture in Kenya.*

1958 Peberday. *Agricultural Gazeteer.*

1963 Brown, L. H. *A National Cash Crop Policy for Kenya* (Part 1).

2. Republic of Kenya

1964 *Kenya Population Census*, 1962.

1966 *Kenya Development Plan*, 1966-70.

1969 *Kenya Development Plan*, 1970-74.

1970 *Eastern Province Regional Physical Development Plan.*

1971 Havelock, Wilfred. "Report of the Working Group on Agricultural Inputs."

1971 *Kenya Population Census*, 1969.

1972 Ambrose, H. B. "The Case for Intensified Agricultural Research for the Medium Potential Areas of Kenya."

1974 *Kenya Development Plan*, 1974-78.

1974 *Employment, Incomes and Equality in Kenya.*

1977 Braun, H. M. H. *Proposal for an Agroclimatological Classification.* Kenya Soil Survey Project.

1977 Machakos District Integrated Development Program (M.I.D.P.), "Submission to the European Economic Community."

1978 Ministry for Lands and Settlement. *Human Settlements in Kenya: A Strategy for Urban and Rural Development.*

1979 *Arid and Semi-arid Lands Development in Kenya: The Framework for Implementation*, Program Planning and Evaluation.

1979 *Kenya Development Plan*, 1979-1983, Summary Review and Analysis.

1979 M.I.D.P. "Brief for the Minister of Cooperative Development During Discussions on MIDP."

1980 M.I.D.P. "Concise Soil and Water Conservation Plan for Kyangala Catchment."

1981 "National Food Policy." Sessional Paper No. 4.

1982 Overseas Development Institute. "Machakos Integrated Development Programme: Phase I Evaluation" (amended 14 December 1982).

1983 M.I.D.P., "Phase II Project Dossier for Submission to the European Economic Community."

1983 Office of the President. "District focus for Rural Development."

1983 *Kenya Development Plan*, 1984-85.

1984 Ministry of Finance and Planning. "Handbook for A.S.A.L. Field Program and Headquarters A.S.A.L. Section Staff."

1984 M.I.D.P., Annual Work Plan, 1984/86.

II. Secondary Sources

A. Books and Monographs

Bates, Robert. 1981. *Markets and States in Tropical Africa*. Berkeley: University of California Press.

Berg, Robert and Jennifer Whitaker, eds. 1986. *Strategies for African Development*. Berkeley: University of California Press.

Bernard, Frank E. 1969. *Recent Agricultural Change East of Mount Kenya*. Athens, Ohio: Ohio University Center of International Studies, Papers in International Studies, Africa Series, No. 4.

Berry, L., et al. 1971. *Pilot Studies of Human Adjustment to Agricultural Drought in Tanzania*. Toronto, Canada: Natural Hazards Research Paper, No. 19.

Bigsten, A. 1980. *Regional Inequality and Development: A Case Study of Kenya*. London: Gower.

Blaikie, P. 1983. *The Political Economy of Soil Erosion*. London: Longmans.

Brett, E. A. 1973. *Colonialism and Underdevelopment in East Africa: The Politics of Economic Change 1919-1939*. New York: Nok Publishers.

Brown, Lester L. and Edward C. Wolf. 1985. *Reversing Africa's Decline*. Washington, D.C.: Worldwatch Publications, No. 65.

Carlson, J. 1980. *Economic and Social Transformation in Rural Kenya*. Uppsala: Scandinavian Institute of African Studies.

Chisholm, Michael. 1962. *Rural Settlement and Land Use*. London: Hutchinson University Library.

Clayton, E. S. 1964. *Agrarian Development in Peasant Societies: Some Examples from Kenya*. London: Pergamon Press.

Cone, L. Winston, and J. F. Lipscomb. 1972. *The History of Kenya Agriculture*. Nairobi: University Press.

DeWilde, J. C. 1967. *Experience with Agricultural Development in Tropical Africa*. 2 vols. Baltimore: Johns Hopkins University Press.

_________. 1984. *Agriculture, Marketing, and in Pricing Sub-Saharan Africa*. Los Angeles: African Studies Association.

Dommen, Arthur J. 1988. *Innovation in African Agriculture*. Boulder, Colorado: Westview Press.

Eicher, Carl. 1986. *Transforming African Agriculture*. The Hunger Project Papers, No. 4. San Francisco.

Feierman, Steven. 1974. *The Shambaa Kingdom*. Madison: The University of Wisconsin Press.

Forbes-Munro, J. 1975. *Colonial Rule and the Kamba*. Oxford: Clarendon Press.

Freeman, Donald B. and Glen B. Norcliffe. 1985. *Rural Enterprise in Kenya*. Chicago: University of Chicago, Department of Geography, Research Paper Series, No. 214.

Goldsmith, F. H. 1955. *John Ainsworth, Pioneer Kenya Administrator, 1864-1946*. London: Macmillan.

Gregory, J. W. 1896. *The Great Rift Valley*. London: John Murray.

Harrison, Paul. 1987. *The Greening of Africa*. London: Earthscan (Penguin Books).

Hart, K. 1982. *The Political Economy of West African Agriculture*. Cambridge: Cambridge University Press.

Hazelwood, Arthur. 1979. *The Economy of Kenya*. New York: Oxford University Press.

Heyer, Judith, D. Ireri, and J. Morris. 1971. *Rural Development in Kenya*. Nairobi: East African Publishing House.

Heyer, Judith, J. K. Maitha, and W. N. Senga. 1976. *Agricultural Development in Kenya: An Economic Assessment*. Nairobi: Oxford University Press.

Heyer, Judith, P. Roberts, and G. Williams. 1981. *Rural Development in Tropical Africa*. London: McMillan.

Hill, Polly. 1986. *Development Economics on Trial*. Cambridge: Cambridge University Press.

Hobley, E. W. 1910. *Ethnography of the Akamba and Other East African Tribes*. Cambridge: University Press.

Huxley, Elsbeth. 1961. *A New Earth, A Experiment in Colonialism*. London: Chatto and Windus.

Hyden, Goran. 1979. *Tanzania After Ujamaa*. Berkeley: University of California Press.

_________. 1983. *No Shortcuts to Progress: African Development Management in Perspective*. London: Heinemann.

International Bank for Reconstruction and Development. 1963. *The Economic Development of Kenya*. Baltimore, Maryland: The Johns Hopkins University Press.

_________. *Kenya: Into the Second Decade*. 1975. Baltimore, Maryland: Johns Hopkins University Press.

Killick, Tony, ed. 1981. *Papers on the Kenyan Economy*. London: Heinemann Educational Books.

Kitching, Gavin. 1980. *Class and Economic Change in Kenya*. New Haven: Yale University Press.

Kjekshus, Helge. 1977. *Ecology Control and Economic Development in East African History*. Berkeley: University of California Press.

Krapf, J. L. 1860. *Travels, Researches, and Missionary Labors in Eastern Africa*. London: Trubner.

Larby, Norman. 1944. *The Kamba*. Nairobi: W. Boyd & Co., The People of Kenya Series, No. 8.

Lele, Uma. 1975. *The Design of Rural Development: Lessons from Africa.* Baltimore: Johns Hopkins University Press.

Leys, Colin. 1974. *Underdevelopment in Kenya: The Political Economy of Neo-Colonialism 1964-1971.* Berkeley: University of California Press.

Liebenow, J. Gus. 1971. *Colonial Rule and Political Development in Tanzania: The Case of the Makonde.* Evanston: Northwestern University Press.

_________. 1986. *African Politics.* Bloomington: University of Indiana Press.

Lindblom, K. G. 1920. *The Akamba of British East Africa.* Uppsala: Appelborgs Boktrycheri Aktieborg.

Mariuki, Godfrey. 1971. *A History of the Kikuyu, 1500-1900.* London: Oxford University Press.

Maxon, R. M. 1980. *John Ainesworth and the Making of Kenya.* New York: University Press of America.

Mbithi, Phillip and Carolyn Barnes. 1975. *Spontaneous Settlement Problems in Kenya.* Nairobi: East African Literature Bureau.

Mbiti, John. 1969. *Akamba Stories.* Oxford: Clarendon Press.

_________. 1971. *New Testament Eschatology in an African Background.* London: Oxford University Press.

Middleton, John. 1953. *The Kikuyu and Kamba of Kenya.* London: International African Institute.

Mitchell, Sir P. 1947. *The Agrarian Problems in Kenya.* Nairobi: Government Printer.

Moris, Jon R. 1981. *Managing Induced Rural Development.* Bloomington, Indiana: International Development Institute.

Murdoch, William. 1980. *The Poverty of Nations: The Political Economy of Development and Underdevelopment.* Baltimore: Johns Hopkins University Press.

Mwaniki, H. S. K. 1973. *The Living History of Embu and Mbeere.* Nairobi: East African Literature Bureau.

Ndeti, Kivuto. 1972. *Elements of Akamba Life*. Nairobi: East African Publishing House.

Norcliffe, Glen and Tom Pinfold. 1981. *Planning African Development*. London: Croom Helm.

Obudho, R. A. 1983. *Urbanization in Kenya*. Lanham, Maryland: University Press of America.

Oliver, Roland, and Gervase Mathew. 1963. *History of East Africa*. London: Oxford University Press.

Orde-Browne, I.St.J. 1925. *The Vanishing Tribes of Kenya*. London: Seeley, Service & Co. Ltd.

Palmer, R. and N. Q. Parsons, eds. 1977. *The Roots of Rural Poverty in Central and Southern Africa*. Berkeley: The University of California Press.

Penwill, D. J. *Kamba Customary Law*. 1951. London: Macmillan & Co.

Porter, Phillip. 1979. *Food and Development in the Semi-Arid Zone of East Africa*. Syracuse: Syracuse University, Foreign and Comparative Studies, African Series, No. 32.

Pratt, D. J. and M. D. Gwynne. 1977. *Rangeland Management and Ecology in East Africa*. Huntington, N.Y.: R. E. Krieger.

Richards, Paul. 1985. *Indigenous Agricultural Revolution*. London: Hutchinson.

_________. 1986. *Coping with Hunger: Hazard and Experimentation in an African Rice-Farming System*. London: Allen & Unwin.

Roberts, A., ed. 1968. *Tanzania Before 1900*. Nairobi: East African Publishing House.

Roscoe, J. 1921. *Twenty-Five Years in East Africa*. Cambridge: Cambridge University Press.

Ruthenberg, Hans. 1966. *Agricultural Policy in Kenya: 1945-1965*. Berlin: Springer-Verlag.

Saberwell, Satish. 1970. *The Traditional Political System of the Embu of Central Kenya*. 1972. Nairobi: East African Publishing House.

Sandbrook, Richard. 1982. *The Politics of Basic Needs*. Toronto: University of Toronto Press.

Seidman, Ann. 1972. *Comparative Development Strategies in East Africa*. Nairobi: East African Publishing House.

Sheffield, James R., ed. 1967. *Education, Employment and Rural Development*. Nairobi: East African Publishing House.

Soja, Edward. 1968. *The Political Modernization of Kenya*. Syracuse: Syracuse University Press.

Thompson, Joseph. 1895. *Through Masailand: A Journey of Exploration Among the Snow Clad Volcanic Mountains and Strange Tribes of Eastern Equatorial Africa*. London: Sampson, Low, Marston & Co.

Tignor, Robert L. 1976. *The Colonial Transformation of Kenya: The Kamba, Kikuyu and Masai from 1900-1939*. Princeton, New Jersey: Princeton University Press.

Timberlake, Lloyd. 1985. *Africa in Crisis*. Washington, D.C.: Earthscan.

Van Zwanenberg, R. M. A. and Ann King. 1975. *An Economic History of Kenya and Uganda: 1800-1970*. London: Macmillan Press.

Watt, Rachael S. 1900. *In the Heart of Savagedom*. London: Marshall Bros. Ltd.

Wolff, R. D. 1974. *The Economics of Colonialism: Kenya and Britain, 1870-1930*. New Haven: Yale University Press.

World Bank. 1981. *Accelerated Development in Sub-saharan Africa, An Agenda for Action*. Washington, D.C.

_________. 1983. *Kenya: Growth and Structural Change*. Washington, D.C.

_________. 1984. *Annual Report*. Washington, D.C.

Yeager, Rodger. 1987. *Africa's Conservation for Development*. Hanover, New Hampshire: The African-Caribbean Institute.

B. Journal Articles, Book Chapters, Dissertations and Papers

Ainesworth, John. 1896. "On a Journey from Machakos to Kitui." *Geographical Magazine* 7:406-12.

Alila, Patrick. 1985. "Administration of Coops for Rural Development in Kenya." In *Challenging Rural Poverty*, ed. Fasil G. Kiros. Trenton, New Jersey: Africa World Press.

Ambler, Charles. 1981. "Movement, Social Formation, and the Evolution of Regional Systems: Central Kenya in the Nineteenth Century." Paper presented at the Annual Meeting, African Studies Association, Washington, D.C.

Arrighi, G. 1973. "Labor Supplies in an Historical Perspective; A Study of the Proletarianization of the African Peasantry in Rhodesia." In *Essays of the Political Economy of Africa*, ed. G. Arrighi and J. S. Saul. New York: Monthly Review Press.

Atieno, Odhiambo, E. S. 1972. "The Rise and Decline of the Kamba Peasant, 1882-1922." *East African Journal* 9:11-15.

Baker, S. J. K. 1974. "A Background to the Study of Drought in East Africa." *African Affairs* 73:170-177.

Barker, David and Alan Ferguson. 1981-82. "The Craft Training Center as a Rural Mobilization Policy in Kenya." *Rural Africana* 13:75-90.

Beidelman, T. 0. 1961. "Some Notes on the Kamba District." *Tanganyika Notes and Records* 53:181-194.

Beresford-Stoke, G. 1929. "An Akamba Ceremony Used in Times of Drought." *Man* 28:139-140.

Bernard, Frank E. and Derrick Thom. 1981. "Population Pressure and Human Carrying Capacity in Selected Locations in Machakos and Kitui District," *Journal of Developing Areas* 15:381-406.

Bernard, Frank. 1985. "Planning and Environmental Risk in the Kenyan Drylands." *Geographical Review* 75:58-70.

Berry, Sara. 1986. "Social Science Perspectives on Food in Africa." In *Food in Sub-Saharan Africa*, ed. Art Hansen and Della E. McMillan. Boulder, Colorado: Lynne Rienner, Publishers.

Blackie, M. 1987. "Restructuring Marketing Systems for Smallholders: Cases in Zimbabwe." In *Accelerating Food Production in Sub-Saharan Africa*, ed. J. Mellor, C. Delgado and M. Blackie. Baltimore: Johns Hopkins University Press, 187-209.

Boninger, James. 1956. "New Ways of Living for Kamba Tribesmen." *Community Development Bulletin* 7:28-30.

Brandstrom, Per. 1985. "Do We Really Learn from Experience? Reflections on Development Efforts in Sukumaland, Tanzania." *Land Management and Survival*, ed. Anders Hjort. Uppsala: Scandinavian Institute of African Studies.

Brown, L. H. 1968. "Agricultural Change in Kenya." *Food Research Institute Studies* 8:33-90.

Buch-Hansen, Mogens and Jan Kieler. 1983. "The Development of Capitalism and the Transformation of the Peasantry in Kenya." *Rural Africana* 15-16:13-40.

Callaghy, T. M. 1988. "Debt and Structural Adjustments in Africa," *Issue* 16, 2:11-18.

Chang, Jen-hu. 1977. "Tropical Agriculture, Crop Diversity and Crop Yields." *Economic Geography* 53:241-254.

Cliffe, Lionel. 1975. "Underdevelopment or Socialism? A Comparative Analysis of Kenya and Tanzania." In *The Political Economy of Africa*, ed. Richard Harris. Cambridge, Mass.: Schenkman Publishing Co.

Cummings, Robert J. 1975. "Aspects of Human Porterage with Special Reference to the Akamba of Kenya: Toward an Economic History 1820-1920." Ph.D. Diss. U.C.L.A., Los Angeles.

Datoo, Bashir A. 1977. "Peasant Agricultural Production in East Africa; The Nature and Consequences of Dependence." *Antipode* 9:70-77.

DeKiewiet-Hemphill, Marie. "The British Sphere, 1884-94." In *History of East Africa*, Vol. 1, ed. Vincent Harlow, and E. M. Chilver. Oxford: Clarendon Press.

Delp, Peter. 1980. "District Planning in Kenya." Harvard Institute for International Development, Discussion Paper No. 95.

Dietz, Jon. 1986. "Migration to and From Dry Areas of Kenya." *Tijdschrift voor Economishe en Sociale Geografie* 77, 1:18-26.

Dresch, Jean. 1975. "Reflections of the Future of Semi-Arid Regions." In *African Environment: Problems and Perspectives*, ed. Paul Richards. International African Institute, Special Report No. 1.

Ehret, Christopher. 1974. "The Nineteenth Century Roots of Economic Imperialism in Kenya." *Kenya Historical Review* 2: 279-284.

Elkan, Walter, and Roger Van Zwanenberg. 1974. "How People Came to Live in Towns." Institute for Development Studies, University of Nairobi, Miscellaneous Paper No. 63.

Fair, T. J. D. 1985. "Kenya: Pressure on the Land." *African Insight* 15:22-25.

Ford, Richard. 1983. "Local Leadership and Local Decisions in Improved Resource Planning and Management." Paper presented at the Workshop on Natural Resource Planning, Clark University.

Gillman, Margaret. 1973. "Concepts of Inter-Tribal Relations on the Kamba-Masai Border." *Kenya Historical Review* 1:33-44.

Grum, Anders. 1971. "Rural Akamba Housing." *Plan East Africa* 11:38-41.

Gwyer, G. D. 1973. "Trends in Kenyan Agriculture in Relation to Employment." *The Journal of Modern African Studies* 2: 393-403.

Gwynne, M. D. 1981. "Issues in the Development of Kenya's Semi-Arid Areas." In *The Development of Kenya's Semi-Arid Lands*, ed. David Campbell and S. E. Migot-Adholla. Institute for Development Studies, University of Nairobi, Occasional Paper No. 36.

Harbeson, J. W. 1970. "Nationalism and Nation-Building in Kenya: The Role of Land Reform." Ph.D. Diss., University of Michigan, Ann Arbor.

Heyer, Judith. 1965. "Seasonal Labor Inputs in Peasant Agriculture." Paper presented at the East African Agricultural Economics Conference, Nairobi.

Heyer, Judith. 1965. "Some Problems in the Valuation of Subsistence Output." Center for Economic Research, University College Nairobi, Discussion Paper No. 14.

_________. 1966. "Alternative Development Strategies for Lowland Machakos Farms." Institute for Development Studies, University of Nairobi, Discussion Paper No. 35.

_________. 1967. "The Economics of Small-Sale Farming in Lowland Machakos." Institute for Development Studies, University of Nairobi, Occasional Paper No. 1.

_________. 1974. "A Survey of Agricultural Development in the Small Farm Areas of Kenya Since the 1920s," Institute for Development Studies, University of Nairobi, Working Paper No. 194.

_________. 1975. "The Origins of Regional Inequalities in Smallholder Agriculture in Kenya, 1920-1973." *Eastern African Journal of Rural Development* 8:122-181.

Hinderink, J. and J. Sterkenburg. 1983. "Agricultural Policy and Production in Africa: The Aims, Methods and Means." *The Journal of Modern African Studies* 21:1-23.

Hobley, C. W. 1912. "Kamba Protective Magic." *Man* 13:4-6.

Holmquist, Frank. 1984. "Self-Help: The State and Peasant Leverage in Kenya." *Africa* 54:72-91.

House, William J. and Tony Killick. 1983. "Social Justice and Development Policy in Kenya's Rural Development." In *Agrarian Policies and Rural Poverty in Africa*, ed. Dharam Ghai and Samir Radwan. Geneva: International Labor Office.

Hunt, Diana. 1977. "Poverty and Agricultural Development Policy in Semi-Arid Area of Eastern Kenya." In *Land Use and Development*, ed. Phil O'Keefe and Ben Wisner. International African Institute, African Environment Special Report No. 5.

Jackson, K. A. 1972. "An Ethno-historical Study of the Oral Traditions of the Akamba of Kenya." Ph.D. Diss., U.C.L.A., Los Angeles.

Jackson, K. A. 1976. "The Dimensions of Kamba Pre-Colonial History." In *Kenya Before 1900*, ed. B. A. Ogot. Nairobi: East African Publishing House.

Jacobs, Donald. 1961. "The Cultural Themes and Puberty Rites of the Akamba, A Bantu Tribe in East Africa." Ph.D. Diss., New York University.

Jamieson, Barbara. 1978. "Resource Allocation to Agricultural Research in Kenya from 1963-1978." Institute for Development Studies, University of Nairobi, Working Paper No. 345.

Johnson, Bruce. 1986. "Government Strategies for Agricultural Development." In *Strategies for African Development*, ed. R. Berg and J. S. Whitaker. Berkeley: University of California Press.

Kimambo, Isaria. 1978. "The Economic History of the Kamba, 1850-1950." In *Hadith 2*, ed. Bethwell A. Ogot. Nairobi: East African Publishing House.

Krokfors, Christer. 1985. "Understanding African Food Situations." In *Land Management and Survival*, ed. Anders Hjort. Uppsala: Scandinavian Institute of African Studies.

Lambert, H. E. 1947. "Land Tenure Among the Akamba." *African Studies* 6:131-147, 157-175.

Lamphear, John. 1970. "The Kamba and the Northern Mrima Coast." In *Pre-Colonial African Trade: Essays on Trade in Central and Eastern Africa Before 1900*. ed. Richard Gray and David Birmingham. London: Oxford University Press.

Lang, Brian. 1970. "Some Aspects of Urbanization in Machakos Township." Institute for Development Studies, University of Nairobi, Discussion Paper No. 3.

Langlands, B. W. 1968. "Factors in Changing Form, Location, and Distribution of Settlements with Particular Reference to East Africa." Institute of Social Research, Makerere University College, Conference Paper No. 2.

Last, J. 1882. "A Journey into the Nguru Country from Mamboia, East Central Africa." *Proceedings of the Royal Geographical Society* 4:148-57.

Leach, J. 1974. "The Kenya Special Rural Development Program." *Journal of Administration Overseas* 13:358-65.

Low, D. A. 1963. "The Northern Interior, 1840-84." *History of East Africa*, Vol. 1, ed. R. 0. Oliver and G. Matthews. Oxford: Clarendon Press.

________. 1965. "British East Africa: The Establishment of British Rule, 1895-1912." In *History of East Africa, Vol. II*, ed. Vincent Harlow and E. M. Chilver. Oxford: Clarendon Press.

Lynam, John K. 1978. "An Analysis of Population Growth, Technological Change and Risk in Peasant, Semi-Arid Farming Systems: A Case Study of Machakos District, Kenya." Ph.D. Diss., Stanford University, Palo Alto, California.

MacArthur, J. D. 1967. "Some Thoughts on Future Trends in Farm Employment in Kenya." In *Education, Employment and Rural Development*, ed. James R. Sheffield. Nairobi: East African Publishing House.

MacKenzie, Fiona and D. R. F. Taylor. 1985. "Regional and Rural Development Strategies: The Case of District Focus in Kenya," Paper presented at the Annual Meeting, Middle States and New England/St. Lawrence Division, Association of American Geographers, Albany, New York.

M'Arimi, A. M. 1977. "The Effect of Some Tillage Methods and Cropping Sequences on Rainfall Conservation in a Semi-Arid area of Eastern Kenya." M.A. Thesis, University of Nairobi.

________. 1978. "The Effects of Certain Tillage Methods and Cropping Systems for Conserving Rainfall in a Semi-Arid Area of Kenya." Institute of Development Studies, University of Nairobi, Occasional Paper No. 27.

Maxon, Robert. 1973. "John Ainsworth and Agricultural Innovation in Kenya." *Kenya Historical Journal* 1:151-162.

Mbithi, Philip M. 1969. "Famine Losses and Innovation." Department of Rural Economy and Extension, Makerere University College, Paper No. 52.

_________. Dec. 1970. "Self-Help as a Strategy for Rural Development: A Case Study." *Proceedings*, Vol. 5, East African Social Science Conference, Dar es Salaam, Tanzania, 262-293.

_________ and Wisner, Ben 1972. "Drought and Famine in Kenya: Magnitude and Attempted Solutions." Institute for Development Studies, University of Nairobi, Discussion Paper No. 144.

_________ and Wisner, Ben. 1972. "Drought in Eastern Kenya: Comparative Observations of Nutritional Status and Farmer Activity at 17 Sites." Institute for Development Studies, University of Nairobi, Discussion Paper No. 167.

Mbogua, John P. 1984. "A Strategy for Secondary Town Development in Kenya." Paper presented at the 9th African Conference on Urbanization in Africa, Dakar, Senegal.

Moore, T. R. 1979. "Land Use and Erosion in the Machakos Hills." *Annals of the Association of American Geographers* 69: 419-431.

Mosley, Paul. 1982. "Kenya in the 1970's: a Review Article." *African Affairs* 81:271-277.

Mutiso, G. C. M. 1972. "Machakos Inter-Ethnic Political Evolution." East African Social Science Conference, Paper No. 55.

_________. 1976. "Kitui: The Ecosystem, Integration and Change." Paper presented at the Seminar on Environment and Poorly Integrated Societies in Africa, Mauritius.

_________. 1977. "Kitui Livestock." Institute for Development Studies, University of Nairobi, Working Paper No. 305.

Myrick, Bismark. 1975. "Colonial Initiatives and Kamba Reaction in Machakos District: The Destocking Issue, 1930-1938." In

Three Aspects of Crisis in Colonial Kenya. Syracuse University, Foreign and Comparative Studies, Eastern Africa Series No. 211.

Nida, Eugene A. 1962. "Akamba Initiation Rites and Cultural Themes." *Practical Anthropology* 9:245-50, 153-55.

Nyamu, P. M. 1970. "Clan Interaction in Matetani Sub-Location 1946-1970: A Case Study in Social Development." University of Nairobi, Research Paper.

Obol-Owit, L. E. C. 1966. "The Changing Pattern of Settlement in Ornea Onyima in East Acholi." Institute for Social Research, Makerere University College, Conference Paper No. 501.

Odhiambo, Atieno. 1972. "The Rise of the Kenya Peasant 1888-1922." *Proceedings of the African Studies Seminar*, University of Edinburgh, 27-37.

Odingo, R. S. 1971. "Settlement and Rural Development in Kenya." In *Studies in East African Geography and Population*, ed. S. H. Ominde. London: Heinemann Educational Books.

Okali, Christine and Berry, Sara. 1985. "Alley Farming in West Africa in a Comparative Perspective." African Studies Center, Boston University, Discussion Paper No. 11.

O'Keefe, P. and Wisner, Ben. 1975. "African Drought--The State of the Game." In *African Environment; Problems and Perspectives*, ed. Paul Richards. International African Institute, African Environment Special Report No. 1.

_________. 1976. "Development of Underdevelopment: A Kenyan Case Study." *African Environment* 2:107-120.

Okumu, John J. 1966. "Kenya, 1900-1930: A Study in Conflict." Ph.D. Diss., U.C.L.A., Los Angeles.

Oliver, Symmes. 1965. "Individuality, Freedom of Choice and Cultural Flexibility." *American Anthropologist* 67:421-428.

Omo-Fadeka, J. 1977. "Development: The Third Way." *African Environment* 2:7-36.

Onchere, Simeon R. and R. Slooff, R. 1981. "Nutrition and Disease in Machakos District, Kenya." In *Seasonal Dimensions of Rural Poverty*, ed. Robert Chambers, Richard Longhurst and Arnold Pacey. London: Allenheld, Osmun & Company.

Owako, F. N. 1965. "Machakos Land and Population Problems." In *Studies in Geography and Development in East Africa*. ed. S. Ominde. London: Heinemann.

_________. 1969. "The Machakos Problem: A Study of Some of the Aspects of the Agrarian Problems of Machakos District, Kenya." Ph.D. Diss., University of London.

Oyugi, Walter Ouma. 1985. "Center-Periphery Linkages in the Development Process: An Assessment of the Kenyan Experience." In *Challenging Rural Poverty*, ed. Fassil G. Kiros. Trenton, New Jersey: Africa World Press.

Palmer, Gary. 1971. "The Shimba Hills Settlement Scheme." Ph.D. Diss., University of Minnesota, Minneapolis.

Penwill, D. J. 1952. "Sub-Chiefs in Kikuyu and Ukambani." Paper presented at the Annual Conference, Institute for Social Research, Makerere University.

Porter, Philip. 1965. "Environmental Potentials and Economic Opportunities: A Background for Cultural Adaptation." *American Anthropologist* 67:409-420.

Raa, Eric Ten. 1968. "Bush Foraging and Agricultural Development: A History of Sandawe Famines." *Tanganyika Notes and Records* 69:33-39.

Roling, Neils, Chege, Fred, and Oscroft, J. 1973. "Rapid Development for Kenya's Small Farms." Institute for Development Studies, University of Nairobi, Discussion Paper No. 73.

Shaatz, John M. and Eicher, Carl. 1986. "Agricultural Development Ideas in Historical Perspective." In *Food in Sub-Saharan Africa*, ed. Art Hansen and Della E. McMillan. Boulder, Colorado: Lynne Rienner Publishers.

Silberfein, Marilyn. 1984. "Differential Development in Machakos District, Kenya." In *Life Before the Drought*, ed. Earl Scott. Winchester, Mass.: Allen and Unwin.

Simiyu, Vincent. 1974. "Land and Politics in Ukambani Kenya from the End of the 19th Century up to 1933." *Presence Africane* 89:101-146.

Smith, L. D. 1976. "An Overview of Agricultural Development Policy." In *Agricultural Development in Kenya*, ed. J. Heyer et al. Nairobi: Oxford University Press.

Stanner, W. E. H. 1939. "The Kitui Kamba: A Critical Account of British Administration and the Kitui Kamba." Ph.D. Diss., University of London.

Tait, David J. "Development of the Small Farm Sector in Kenya: 1954-72." *Canadian Geographer* 21:32-57.

Tate, H. R. 1904. "Notes on the Kikuyu and Kamba Tribes of British East Africa." *Journal of the Royal Anthropological Institute* 34:130-148.

Taylor, D. R. F. 1969. "Agricultural Change in Kikuyuland." In *Environment and Land Use in Africa*, ed. M. F. Thomas and W. G. Withington. London: Methuen.

_________. 1974. "Spatial Aspects of Kenya's Rural Development Strategy." In *Spatial Aspects of Development*, ed. B. S. Hoyle. New York: John Wiley and Sons.

ter Kuile, Coenrad. 1987. "The Humid and Subhumid Tropics." In *Accelerating Food Production in Sub-Saharan Africa*, ed. J. Mellor, C. Delgado, and M. Blackie. Baltimore: Johns Hopkins University Press.

Thom, Derick and Niels L. Martin. 1983. "Ecology and Production in Baringo-Kerio Valley, Kenya." *Geographical Review* 73:15-29.

Thomas, Anthony E. June, 1969. "Community Adaptation to Health Services in the Machakos District of Kenya: A Preliminary Report." Institute for Development Studies, University of Nairobi, Staff Paper No. 36.

Ueda, Hitoshi. 1973. "Witchcraft and Sorcery in Kitui Kamba Tribes." East African Studies, University of Nairobi, Discussion Paper No. 25.

Van Ginneken, J. K., Omondi-Odhiambo, and A. S. Muller. 1986. "Mobility Patterns in a Rural Area of Machakos District, Kenya in 1974-1980." *Tijdscrift voor Economishe and Sociale Geografie* 77:82-91.

Van Zwanenberg, R. 1974. "The Development of Peasant Production in Kenya, 1920-42." *The Economic History Review*, 2nd Series, 27:442-454.

Watts, Michael and Thomas Bassett. 1985. "Crisis and Change in African Agriculture: A Comparative Study of the Ivory Coast and Nigeria." *African Studies Review* 28:3-27.

Wisner, Ben. 1976. "Man-Made Famine in Eastern Kenya: The Interrelationship of Environment and Development." University of Sussex, Institute for Development Studies, Discussion Paper No. 96.

_________. 1976. "An Overview of Drought in Kenya." Natural Hazards Research, Boulder, Colorado, Working Paper No. 30.

_________. 1977. "Constriction of the Livelihood System: The Peasants of Tharaka Division, Meru District, Kenya." *Economic Geography* 53:353-357.

_________. 1977. "Man-Made Famine in Eastern Kenya: The Interrelationship of Environment and Development." In *Land Use and Development*, ed. Phil O'Keefe and Ben Wisner. International African Institute, African Environment Special Report No. 5.

Wisner, Ben. 1977. "The Human Ecology of Drought in Eastern Kenya." Ph.D. Diss., Clark University, Worcester, Mass.

Wood, A. P. 1976. "Farmers' Responses to Drought in Ethiopia." In *Drought and Famine in Ethiopia*, ed. Abdul Mejid Hussein. International African Institute, African Environment Special Report No. 2.

Wood, Joseph, and C. Gregory Knight. 1975. "Cross-Cultural Perspectives on Human Adjustments to Arid Margins." In *Drought, Famine and Population Movements in Africa*, ed. James Newman. Syracuse University, East Africa Series, No. 17.

Zende, Bahru. 1976. "A Historical Outline of Famine in Ethiopia. In *Drought and Famine in Ethiopia*, ed. Abdul Majid

Hussein. International African Institute, African Environment Special Report No. 2.

C. Reports

1. United States Agency for International Development (USAID)

1975 Johnson, W., Berry, Len, Abercrombie, Frank. "Pre-Investment Study of Agricultural Potential of Marginal Semi-Arid Lands of Kenya." Revised Draft and Scope of Work.

1978 Palmer, Byron et al. "Kenya: Arid and Semi-Arid Lands Pre-Investment Inventory." Washington D.C. 10 volumes.

Report No. 2, Mann, Herbert. "Agronomy."
Report No. 3, Hash, Charles and Mbatha, Bernard. "Economics."
Report No. 4, Daines, S. H., Njorage, Paula and Njui, Karanga. "Soil and Water Management."
Report No. 6, Thom, Derrick. "Human Resources and Social Characteristics."

1978 Nadar, Hassan M. and Gordon Rodewald. "Katumani Maize and the Long Rains in the Machakos Area."

1981 Meyers, L. Richard. "Organization and Administration of Integrated Rural Development in Semi-Arid Areas: The Machakos Integrated Development Program."

1982 Fleuret, P. and Ned Greeley. "The Kenya Social and Institutional Profile." Kenya Program Office.

1985 "Country Development Strategy Statement."

2. United Nations, International Labor Office (ILO)

1972 "Employment, Incomes and Equality: A Strategy for Increasing Productive Employment in Kenya."

1981 Livingstone, Ian. "Rural Development, Incomes and Employment in Kenya."

INDEX

ABOUT THE AUTHOR

Marilyn Silberfein is an Associate Professor of Geography and Urban Studies at Temple University in Philadelphia, Pa. She received both her M.A. and Ph.D. at Syracuse University. For the past fifteen years she has alternated between teaching and doing field work in Africa with grants from the National Geographic Society, Social Science Research Council, and Fulbright Program. She also spent two years working for the U.S. Agency for International Development in Washington, D.C. and on overseas assignments.

Dr. Silberfein has published monographs, articles and book chapters on rural development. Her major research themes include adaptations to a semi-arid environment and the importance of settlement types and of small towns in stimulating rural growth. She is currently becoming involved in a U.S. based initiatives: the nation-wide effort to promote geographical education.